THE
HOME BUYER
BLUEPRINT:

7 Keys to Start Building Wealth

By

Chad Murray

ISBN:978-1-7334196-2-8

Scan the QR Code below to set up a home buying consultation or email: hello@chadthelender.com

For access to the worksheets throughout the book, you will find a different QR code than above on each worksheet. That QR Code will give you access to all worksheets in this book.

Dedication

This book is dedicated to my entire family. I am blessed beyond measure to be of this tribe. I wouldn't be where I am today without my parents, my children, my siblings, cousins, nieces and nephews, and the elders and ancestors who have guided my path.

May God continue to bless you all and bless me with you all.

Other Titles by Chad Murray:

- *The Credit Building Blueprint*
- *Give Your$elf Credit: Your Financial Lifestyle Planner*
- *The Credit Boosting Blueprint* (DIY Course)
- *Home Buyer's Academy* (Online course)
- Home Buyer's Academy Challenge (Coaching program/Home buying challenge)

Acknowledgements

I'm extremely blessed to have the support of the following people who were instrumental in me completing this project in excellence.

Thank you, Mommy, for being a one-woman support system. You've been there for every great and not-so-great event in my life and loved me through it all.

Thank you, Daddy, for giving me the confidence which makes me feel like I'm 10 feet tall.

My sisters and brother, you all have been the iron who sharpens my iron. To have my best advisors know me and love me the way you do makes my life fulfilled.

Acknowledgements

To Betty Norlin, I'm so grateful for your patience and diligence in working on this book with me. You've worked with me through a particularly challenging time in my life and I truly appreciate all you have been for me.

Shakira Thompson, you are absolutely brilliant and I'm so fortunate to be able to tap into your well of genius ideas and perspectives.

The Murray/Campbell family. You've given me a second mom, dad, brothers, a sister, and nieces and nephews, and love unlimited. How am I so lucky to have you all?

Thank you to Kim Givens and Florence Saint-Jean for sparking this book into action through our mastermind. I knew I wanted to write this book but without you I would not have done it, yet.

Thank you, Lesley Almonte, for helping me to create the resources for this book that will help so many people. You are truly a visionary.

Jimmy Leo, you're my brother, and I'm grateful for your steadfast support. Being able to bounce the ideas in this book off you helped me more than you know.

Thank you to everyone who allowed me to interview them for "The Blueprints" and to share their expertise in real estate. I'm truly grateful to you all. I want to give a big thank you to my newest brother Maurice Jones for taking the time to give me great insights on how to make this project even better. I think we did it bro!

I'm honored to have my NAREB family and the Urban League in Central Florida, New York, and across the country to be the boots on the ground in this journey to open the gates of homeownership to more people in more communities.

There are so many other people who have been crucial to bringing this book to life and I am eternally grateful to all of you.

Table of Contents

Introduction

It felt like the saddest day ever. It was the middle of the school year and my sister Atiya, and I, had to say tear filled goodbyes to all our friends in Turtle Hook Junior High school. We were in 8th grade, and we were moving again! The friendships we developed, our classes, clubs, and the basketball team that I finally made, all were ripped out of our lives without having a say in the matter. We were whisked away across town to the rival middle school Lawrence Road Junior High School. Atiya, my Irish-twin sister, and I were so mad at Mommy and Daddy but what could we do? This was the fourth time in eight years we had to start over.

Despite their best motives, parents often make decisions which deeply hurt their children's lives.

Their inability to provide a stable home can lead to long lasting and generational scars that may never get fixed. Luckily for my four sisters and I, my mother and father gave us so much love, so we never felt the brunt of the storms that constantly hit our living situation. Even more importantly, we always had "Granny's House."

My grandmother and grandfather migrated to America from Trinidad and Tobago in the West Indies. They bought their first house in Brooklyn, NY and later bought another in Uniondale, on Long Island, New York, where my mother, (sometimes my fathers), siblings, and I ended up time and again after failed attempts to maintain a home. We moved a lot! But we never really felt unstable because of "Granny's House." It was the biggest house on a small dead-end block. The backyard felt huge, and our friends were a jump of a fence away on each side.

At times there were as many as 10 of us living under one roof with my aunt and my little cousins at the time helping us to be as snug as possible. Being children, we weren't privy to the arguments about the congestion, and groceries, and bills. All we knew was every weekend felt like a block party with Double Dutch, baseball games, and neighbor-hood wide games of hide and seek in the dark, illuminated by fireflies.

Introduction

As kids, we couldn't be happier with our childhood, but my mother felt like she let us down because we were always temporary guests in other people's homes. From "Granny's House" to renting a house, to "Granny's House" again. That's what it was. What my mother didn't realize at the time was "Granny's House" was the cornerstone of many houses to come for our family.

Homeownership is never about the brick and mortar that makes a house. It's about the families, memories, and legacies built once you sign on that line. Wealth passes through families in large part by the real estate which has gone from parents to children. One house can turn into down payments for a few houses, which can eventually turn into generational wealth. Some families are in their 6th or 7th generation amassing wealth through real estate, while others are at least a generation away from getting their first property. This is an enormous gap in wealth.

The purpose of this book is to educate and empower people who have not been blessed with the knowledge of how to buy real estate. This is a step-by-step guide outlining where to start, what to do, and what missteps to avoid. Some people are ready to buy a house today, but don't know it because they don't have the information. Others can get themselves prepared to buy by using this information. Regardless of where they may be, a future homeowner now has the vehicle that can drive him or her to the front door of their first house.

The process of becoming a homeowner is told through the stories of what clients have overcome to achieve their goal. That's all this journey is. An exercise in achieving your goal no matter the challenge, limitation, or limiting belief. I assure you, if the people here can do it, you can do it too. See yourself in them. Whether it took three months or three years like some did, the mission ends with keys, a new home, and a place for a new story to start.

Generational wealth building is the motivation for some, while others see a memory making domain which makes Christmas, Thanksgiving, and birthdays way more special. What drives you to make this happen for you and your family? Being clear on this is the starting point which makes all the rest possible. Each of the "Blueprints" to come start with a "Why."

For Granny, her and my grandfathers "Why" was to build a foundation for their children to make a great life for themselves and to give them more than she had growing up.

CHAPTER 1

Unlocking Your Home Buyer's Mindset

It had been a bumpy road to get to this point, but her landlord was about to make that all change. Michelle and her three children had been living in a big comfortable house on Long Island, NY for two years. They'd finally been able to have a place that felt like home. A couple years back, Michelle went through an ugly divorce and the house she had with her ex-husband was foreclosed on. She went from being a homeowner to a tenant and the children took the transition hard. Now things were finally feeling settled when her landlord said, "I want to sell the house and if you cannot buy it, then you'll have to leave."

Here's where my story with Michelle starts. She reached out to me to get help with her credit so she could buy the house. Her credit was poor because of the foreclosure she experienced. I kept it real with her. "Michelle, there's no way you're going to be able to close on this house unless you work hard and urgently to address all the issues standing in your way to homeownership."

When I say, "all the issues," she had, "all the issues." Foreclosure on her credit, low credit score, and worst of all, not enough money for a down payment. From the first phone call, I knew Michelle was going to buy the house. The work she was about to go through was worth it to her because of her "WHY" for doing it.

Michelle explained to me how she was the mother of three even though she only gave birth to one of them. She adopted two of her children. She had to fight the system to take them out of the foster care system where they'd been neglected and lacking a mother's love. "They've been through too much for me not to go through everything I can to provide them a home." She was clear. Everything she was asked to do to improve her credit, she did it. Everything she was asked to do to close on her mortgage, she did it. Her "WHY" was too strong to quit. Along the process, she was told that she couldn't get the loan because her credit score was too low. She called all her friends and relatives until one of them put her on their credit card as an authorized user. This helped her score go up over 20 points. She was told she did not have enough money for a down payment so she called up everyone she could to do odd jobs and services which got her a good chunk of the money. She was willing to do anything she had to in order for this dream to become a reality.

Unlike Michelle, many homebuyers pack in their dreams and go back to renting at the first sign showing this won't be a cake walk. Credit issues, debt-to-income challenges, and a lack of a down payment are the main reasons 'would be' homeowners give up. These challenges can be significant hurdles for anyone. The difference between people who eventually succeed and those who pay off someone else's mortgage for the next decade is the willingness to go through the process.

Your journey may not be easy. It may not always seem possible, but it is possible. Whether you are self-employed or just coming out of bankruptcy, there is a blueprint for you. For people who have a challenge in their home buying process, it is important to identify those specific elements to address them and move past them.

FIND YOUR "WHY"

What is the most important thing in your life? What do you love doing?

Why is it important to you? Why do you love doing it?

What is your definition of success?

Why would you say that? Can you keep drilling down?

Creating Wealth with Real Estate

In his hit book *Rich Dad Poor Dad* Robert Kiyosaki teaches about the two father figures in his life. His father who was a well-respected professor in Hawaii and his friend's father and mentor who was a successful real estate investor. As a professor, Robert's father made good money. Yet, unless he got a raise, his income would stay the same since there were no more hours for him to work. There were no more days to be added to a week. His "Rich Dad" on the other hand was able to generate more income and equity with every property he bought.

This is the power of real estate.

Real estate is a unique tool that offers multiple vehicles to wealth on the same properties. As discussed earlier, you can gain wealth in real estate by having the value of the property increase through appreciation—and have the amount owed decrease in time with payments made. Building equity turns your house into a savings account that can grow as high as the property value can grow. Another way to build wealth through your property is by generating cash flow. Cash flow is the difference between the monthly housing expenses and the rent the property owner collects each month. If there is money going into your bank after monthly housing expenses are paid, then you have a positive cash flow.

Cash flow represents a residual income stream that grows as property owners increase rents or reduce monthly housing expenses. The greatest part about having a property generate positive cash flow is once you set it up and have the property managed, you no longer have to do anything to make that income come in! This is called "Passive Income."

All kinds of options and wealth are available to you through buying real estate. You can flip properties like in the reality TV shows. You can rent out properties. You can develop land. You can buy apartment buildings, and so much more. It starts with successfully completing the home buying process once. It is not required, but the first home turns into so much more.

If all these other ideas about generating wealth for yourself and for your family sound too far-fetched, consider what can happen when someone buys one house.

I was marketing for motivated sellers who would sell their property at a discounted price when I got a call from Harold. His father recently passed away, so he and his siblings were looking to sell the house quickly. It was something I could do. What I couldn't do was match the price they truly wanted for the house. I made my offer, but they turned me down. Several months later I called to see if they ever sold it. Not only were they able to sell it for top dollar, but each of the siblings walked away with a modest inheritance. Three of the siblings turned around and used that money as a down payment on a house. One invested into a business.

From having one house in the family, three of the owner's children bought houses of their own and another became an entrepreneur. Paying rent keeps a roof over your head but paying on your home ensures the foundation to your legacy. Harold's parents had left a legacy which grew exponentially out of one home. This is what is available to those who get committed to this path. Challenges to this goal will come up, but each issue has a solution one can overcome with proper planning and persistence.

Setting Your Home Buying Goal

The difference between a goal and a wish is one is written down with a date for it to be completed. The other is an idea that can fade away when a new idea comes along. To make the home buying journey a goal, write it down with a date to accomplish it.

There are different stages of the home buying process. Future home buyers can have different goals. Credit is an obstacle for some people when they start their process. One possible goal could be to improve a credit score to 640 by a certain time. For another buyer the challenge can be income. If they do not make enough money to qualify for the home fitting their needs, they could set a goal to increase their income by $10,000 or more in six months.

What the goal is for a buyer's path is specific to where he or she is and what he or she wants. What is true for all buyers is if you write down the specific goals you will significantly increase the likelihood of that goal coming through.

The S.M.A.R.T. Goal method is a process that allows you to break down your goals into the core elements which bring the goal to life.

Creating wealth can be one of those goals. Buying real estate can position your family for wealth with just one house. If your family starts with one house, the chances of your children buying a house goes up. Homeowners build equity over time as they pay their mortgage. As the balance decreases and the value goes up, they earn equity which is the difference between the value of the property and what is owed on the house. Equity is like a savings account put away in your home. Home prices have increased by an average of 3.8% per year over the past 10 years. This means a home purchased 10 years ago could be worth over 38% more today than what it was bought for 10 years ago. With the balance of the mortgage decreasing as mortgage

Unlocking Your Home Buyer's Mindset

S.M.A.R.T. GOALS

S Specific	What is your goal?
M Measurable	How will you know when you reach it?
A Attainable	How will you reach it?
R Realistic	Is it really worth it... and why?
T Time-Bound	When will you accomplish it?

payments are made, your equity is likely to grow significantly in that period.

Rent vs. Homeownership

The transition from being a renter to being an owner comes with a change of outlook. Tenants are in the cash flow business. Only they're on the wrong side of the table.

In the time frame a tenant is renting a house, the landlord is having their expenses paid and equity built up all on the tenant's dollar. Is the landlord immoral for this? OF COURSE NOT! Most people spend their lives working for someone else. This is ultimately the same thing. Like a worker who will put 40 hours of their life in every week. When the company is going through a growth phase where the money is pouring in, does the worker participate in that win? No, they generally don't. They may get a raise if their work is exceptional, but by and large, a win for the company is a win for the company, not its workers.

In real estate, the homeowner is like the company and the tenant is like the worker. The worker or tenant can secure a decent situation for themselves but at no point do they control their lives. If the boss says, "you need to work on weekends" then you'll be working on weekends if you want to keep your job. If the landlord says you cannot play music after 10 pm, then it will be headphones or no music after 10 pm. Most importantly, like the worker who doesn't gain as the company grows, the tenant doesn't earn any equity, even if they're paying the landlord's mortgage and then some.

Having a place to call home is a blessing. Having a home, you own is a blessing to you and your legacy. Homeowners build wealth, while tenants give their wealth away. For those who want to gain wealth and not give it away, it's vital to see what it would take monthly to make the step up. Rental prices have increased so much so, it's not uncommon for a tenant to be paying as much in rent as they would have to pay for a mortgage. Even if it would cost more to own, how much more? How much more are you willing to pay to go from tenant to owner?

Money matters when the discussion is about homeownership. When you think of what you and your family could achieve with $360,000 over 30 years, you can imagine a higher level for your bloodline. Then why aren't more people home-owners? For example, in the African American community only 45.1% of adults are homeowners according to the U.S Census Bureau for 2021. White Americans own at a rate of 71.9%. The huge gap in homeownership rates exists because of our country's history of racial injustice and unrelenting socio-economic disparities.

RENT VS HOME OWNERSHIP COMPARISON

Rental Costs:	
Monthly Rent Cost	
Monthly Utilities	
Insurance - Monthly Payment	
Other (Essential Fix-ups, Furnishing , Etc.)	
Total Monthly Costs Of Renting	
Home Ownership Costs:	
Monthly Mortgage Payment	
Interest Rate Of Mortgage	
Length Of Mortgage - In Years	
Property Taxes	
Pmi	
Insurance - Monthly Payment	
Utilities	
Maintenance/repairs	
Homeowner Association Fees	
Other	
Total Monthly Cost Of Owning	
Monthly Cost Difference Between Renting And Owning	
Upfront Costs Of Ownership	
House Purchase Price	
Down Payment (Assumes 20% Down Payment)	
Closing Costs	
Mortgage Points	
Other (Essential Fix-ups, Furnishing, Etc.)	
Total Upfront Costs Of Ownership	

Understanding this as the status quo, the path to improving the outcomes for homeownership in black communities will be laid out on an individual basis with elements of structural change.

It starts with belief. For two years I volunteered with organizations doing home buying workshops. Attendees would get a certificate making them eligible for down payment assistance. Once a month they would have a room full of wide-eyed students ready to learn and get the down payment money for their homes. There would be community partners from banks, realtors, and a host of real estate professionals volunteering their time and expertise to helping people get uplifted into real estate. The information was consistently amazing and thorough, but after eight hours, the participants rarely acted. They had a certificate in some cases for up to $35,000 toward closing on their home but very few scheduled a mortgage or credit consultation to take the next step. The participants gave up eight hours out of their Saturday, got down payment assistance certificates, and only a small percentage of the attendees ever claimed their down payment and their home.

Why is that? Was it because the program was insufficient? Not at all. The best real estate and finance professionals came out every month to pour into attendees. They volunteered their time and expertise. There was consistent follow-up, and all the resources for homeownership were made available. From what I saw, it was the belief factor. Most of the people came into the class optimistic about the process. By the time the day was over, many of them felt like this was too big of a task. How were they going to fix their credit, save money, and find the people they could trust throughout the journey?

Home buyer programs around the country are facing similar results. The target audience by-in-large do not believe they are eligible to become homeowners. Many of these attendees are the first ones in their family to take this path. Since most of them have not seen it modeled, it requires a great deal of faith and drive to make this a reality.

Buying your house is about transforming your mentality from a tenant to a homeowner mindset.

Michelle had to embrace being a tenant after she lost her first house. Because of that loss, she had a different level of focus to become a homeowner again. As the challenges mounted up, so did her resolve to make it happen. She was diligent about addressing one issue after the other until challenges eventually decided to bother someone else. She got into a credit restoration program that helped her increase her credit score. She did everything from babysitting to doing taxes on the side to get money for a down payment, and she did it all like her children's future depended on it. In fact, the children's futures did depend on it.

- The graduation rate for children of homeowners is 19 percent higher than for renters, and they are twice as likely to acquire some postsecondary education, according to a study in a journal published by the Federal Reserve Bank of New York.

- A 2014 study by the Federal Reserve Bank of Boston of homes with a student about to enter college found that a modest increase in home value for homeowners led to an increase in the child's earnings later in life, while an increase in a property's value for renters led to a decrease in the child's earnings.

"A safe, decent, affordable home is like a vaccine," Dr. Megan Sandel of the Boston University School of Medicine testified to Congress in 2007. "It literally prevents disease. A safe home can prevent mental health and developmental problems, a decent home may prevent asthma or lead poisoning, and an affordable home can prevent stunted growth and unnecessary hospitalizations."

According to these points, the children's futures did depend on it. Knowing these statistics and data points, what would it be worth to your family to own a home?

For Michelle, she dedicated time, money, and every resource she had to become a homeowner. When she signed on the line to complete the closing, she was almost in tears because she knew she had reclaimed her life and given life to the children who look to her every day. She did it! She bought a home against all odds. Since then, the real estate market has experienced a surge in home prices nationwide and she has built a significant amount of equity when before all she had was debt.

Buying real estate is a life changing experience if you stay on the path.

The difference between the Homeowner vs. Tenant Mindset is eye opening. A homeowner looks at repairs, community, schools, and responsibility. For a tenant—no responsibility, no reward!

Things to consider as a homeowner you don't have to do as a tenant:

- Landscaping
- Property taxes
- School district (matters more)
- Renovation and repairs (you don't have to, and you don't get to as a tenant)

20

Unlocking Your Home Buyer's Mindset

DREAM HOME CHECKLIST

Write And Rate Your Preferences 3 - Extremely Important; 2 - Pretty Important 1 - Take It Or Leave It; 0 - Not Important At All		
Location	**Preferences**	**Rating**
Neighborhood		
Schools And School District		
Near Public Transportation		
Near The Airport		
Near The Expressway		
Near Shopping		
Great View		
Type Of Home		
Single-family/ Condo/townhouse		
Property Age (Minimum/maximum)		
Willing To Renovate		
Architectural Style		
Open Floor Plan		
Size And Makeup		
Minimum # Of Bedrooms		
Minumum # Of Bathrooms		
Eat-in-kitchen		
Family Room		
Formal Dining Room		
Formal Living Room		

Blueprint 1

Buying in a Hot Market
Dwain and Jenelle

When my father would come home from work, some days he'd have a plate of food. When he felt my sisters and me hovering over his shoulders he'd say, "All who beg, nah get, all who nuh beg, don't want" in his Jamaican accent. We were screwed! If we wanted food and asked, he was probably going to say no. If we didn't ask, we would not get any of his food.

That's kind of what making an offer is like in a competitive market. If you don't make an offer, you won't buy a property, and even if you do make an offer, you still may not get what you want. This is what Dwain and Jenelle were going through. They started looking for their house in October 2016 yet did not close until June 2017.

I asked them what it was like when they fell in love with a house but didn't get it.

"I'm in my feelings to this day," Jenelle recalls. "The house was perfect and had everything. We made an offer right away. We were so close and at the last minute someone came in with an offer we couldn't compete with, and we lost it." I could see the disappointment on her face. She continued, "I used to drive by it like this could've been my house!"

"Even though that didn't work out, I love my home." Dwain went on to talk about how at first they would go out and look at two to three properties a week. "As the market got more competitive and we got more motivated to buy, we would go out almost every day and sometimes see two or three houses in a day."

They even had to live with relatives for two months because their lease expired.

"We thought about renting, and then moving again, but that would've been a waste of a deposit," said Jenelle. They were really beginning to get discouraged with the whole process. They'd been looking at houses like they were Realtors and with offer after offer, they still didn't get one accepted.

Living with your in-laws couldn't be too easy for Dwain, and as they got close to hitting the wall, they got two offers accepted on the same day. They went from not knowing what to do next to having options! Dwain and Jenelle got married in May and closed on their house in June. Now that's a great Spring!

When I asked, "why are you happy to be homeowners?" Dwain responded, "for one, our house is worth way more than what we bought it for. This market has been crazy and I'm glad we don't have to search anymore." They also felt like it was comforting knowing the mortgage "is what it is, unlike rent which always goes up."

Jenelle added, "Nobody taught me that I should buy a house, much less how. At the time, I just made a career shift and was just starting over. I wasn't making much but together with my husband; our income was just enough. Thankfully we got into the house. I was able to get a better job. My husband and I are thriving and our house keeps going up in value. Getting in the house was the most important thing. Since we've bought our house, we have really been able to build our careers and our lives together." They've also added to the family with a beautiful baby girl!

Homeownership has totally changed the game for the Jenelle and Dwain. They have a house, they're building equity, and they're building their career. When they choose, their house can be a launchpad to build more wealth and more memories.

Blueprint for Buying in a Hot Market

1. Schedule time to see a minimum number of houses each week.
2. Be friendly and relatable to the seller and their agent.
3. Be willing to submit full price offers on multiple houses and move quickly on the houses you like.
4. Make your offer attractive by removing all clauses except for an inspection and appraisal contingencies.
5. Be persistent and consistent and you will find your home.

CHAPTER 2

Unlocking and Building Credit

The average sales price of a new home in 2020 was $389,400 according to statistica.com. This is a lot of money to save to buy a house. The housing market would look a lot different if credit did not exist. Instead, home buyers can leverage their payment history to prove one is trustworthy enough to be given a substantial loan.

For some people, credit is a four-letter word. It's not a curse, it's a blessing, if you understand how to use it. While most people think this is the biggest barrier to achieving homeownership, it is the easiest of all the home buying issues to fix. Look at it this way. If someone doesn't have enough money to put down on a house, then they must wait until they save up enough money or hope their fairy Godmother comes through in the clutch with a significant gift of funds. If someone doesn't make enough money to qualify for a home, they must seek new employment and wait for two years for that income to be counted to attain a loan. If someone is self-employed, their income may not be sufficient unless they claim more money than they would on their taxes and pay a much larger tax bill.

These are common and deal breaking issues that can keep people out of the home buying process for a significant amount of time. Most credit issues on the other hand have solutions that can have someone go from tenant to homeowner in little time. When I bought my first home I had very little credit which was preventing me from getting approved for a home. Becoming a homeowner at 21 years old was not on my radar, yet one day someone came to me and said, "this lady is going into foreclosure and wants to sell before she loses the house. She will sell it for what she owes." My ears perked up.

When I did the numbers, I saw this as a great opportunity for me to make an investment that would be positive from day one. I had the income, the down payment, and the seller was ready. Only I didn't have enough credit. I thought of everything I could to build credit quickly, but I was not having any luck and I was running out of time. Then I remembered my grandfather had excellent credit and if he would add me to one of those credit cards, I would now have another line of credit on my report, perfect payment history, and a very low balance compared to what was owed. This was a perfect credit cocktail.

Within weeks of my grandfather adding me to his card, my credit score skyrocketed, and I had just enough credit history to qualify for a mortgage and buy my first home. With a family member or friend, this could be the "EZ Pass" to better credit. I mention this story not because I advocate for everybody using this method. The purpose is to highlight how quickly credit can be turned from a burden to a blessing.

Credit can be improved by several techniques, strategies, and principles. The key to understanding how they all impact a FICO score is by understanding the algorithm by which scores are derived.

A FICO score is like a report card grade for credit. It ranges from 350-850. The FICO score has many different models which are based on the institution requesting the score. There are also other credit scoring models that are popular, but the FICO model is the most common one.

Credit bureaus collect exhaustive data on people. They get information on where you have lived, worked, and your finances including banking information and debt. Every time you make or miss a payment, the data is purchased by credit bureaus and sold to credit card companies and financial institutions. Based on five key factors, a credit score is produced.

FIVE CREDIT FACTORS

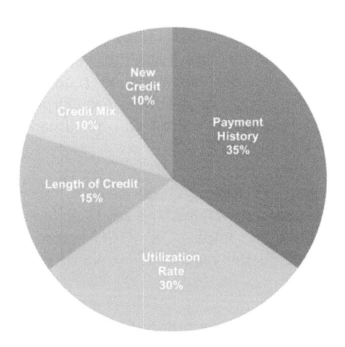

Five Credit Factors

A high FICO score reflects a consumer who demonstrates financial responsibility. The areas particularly most impactful are payment history, utilization rate (the amount of credit owed), length of credit history, credit mix, and new credit. Each one of these factors can have an impact on if a buyer can finance a home or not.

Payment History

Payment history accounts for 35% of a FICO score. If a consumer is late on one payment for over 30 days, it could have a catastrophic impact on their timeline for buying a house. On the other hand, if they are consistent with payments and always make them on time, a home buyer is already more than a third of the way to having excellent credit. In many cases, just making payments on time can have someone in the ballpark of meeting the credit score limit requirements. This part of the equation is the most important as it can make or break one's eligibility for a mortgage.

Since having good credit is vital to a successful home buying journey, it is important to do everything possible to give yourself the best chance of having credit work for you. Why do people miss payments? It can be the loss of a job or income, health issues, or family problems. Things outside of your control can alter your finances. There are many other situations where people are missing payments because they are mismanaging their money or time. This can show up in people overextending themselves with debt, spending more than they're bringing in, and flat out forgetting to pay bills on time.

Credit is a powerful tool, but many people use it as a crutch. They have developed a habit of buying things they don't need to impress people they don't even like! Below are some practices one can use to ensure payment history is working in their favor.

Use the monthly budgeting tool to track your spending and your income. This way you can tell your money where to go rather than wondering where it went. Setting goals is a keyway to manifest the things you want into your life. Budgeting is a form of goal setting, so this process won't just help you with the numbers. It will help you with a plan to achieve your goal.

Automate Payments

Once you know where your money is and when it's going to be there, you can set up automatic withdrawals for your credit cards, auto loans, and other bills. Start with the smallest accounts to make sure your payment due dates and your income cycle are aligned.

Schedule Payments/Alerts

Receive an email, text message, or app alert when your payments are coming up. If you use your daily calendar, you can have an email or text message sent to you either on the due date or prior to the due date based on what you need to stay on track. You can even set multiple alerts or reminders beyond the initial one. There are also apps you can use to set alerts and reminders. We can all use a little help sometimes. If you need help remembering to make a payment, these are tools that are easily accessible to help you.

Utilization Rate

The Credit Utilization Rate is the ratio between how much credit you have available, and how much credit is used. Ultimately, the more credit used from what's available to you, the higher risk you are. The higher the risk you are, the lower your credit score. On the other hand, the more credit you have available, and the less of it you use, the better off for your credit.

The optimal range is to be below 10% of your utilization rate. Having a 30% utilization rate will still lead to a positive credit rating but beyond that, credit scores will begin to stagnate and decline. If you have $1,000 worth of credit available to you, and $200 is used, that credit line has a 20% utilization rate.

The utilization rate is responsible for 30% of a credit score. This credit factor empowers consumers to make a significant impact on their credit in a short period of time. If someone goes on a spending spree using their credit cards, they can cause their FICO score to drop drastically within 30 days. In the same vein, if you reduce credit utilization from 80% usage to 10% usage, you will see a dramatic increase in the credit score. Other areas of credit don't give consumers as much power in the short term. For example, if someone is over 30 days late on a car payment, there's nothing to undo the immediate impact of that delinquency. The credit will only improve after payments are made on time for several months.

With credit utilization, there are a few things you can do to make sure you are always in the best standing possible. With over 30% of a balance being carried, there will be significant amounts of interest being paid. While many chase the benefits of having a high credit score, high balances mean that you are being charged interest on top of interest. From a financial standpoint, this kind of debt can be some of the biggest detractors from wealth.

The primary strategy which works for credit utilization is self-discipline. Spending on credit has become a common and destructive pastime for American consumers. As credit balances get bigger, other financial dreams fade away. Saving money, investing, and more become much harder because of the high interest rates that credit card companies charge. This is a spending problem. Therefore, the best way to fix it is to stop spending on credit. Unfortunately, many people have developed a dependency on credit cards. Having to stop using them is a complete financial shift from the habit that they have developed. To make a change in this area of life, sacrifice is needed and is well worth it.

The next strategy to improve credit utilization is through the Debt Snowball debt payment method. This strategy has been made famous by many financial coaches. The way it works is explained below.

Step 1:
List out all revolving credit you have.

Step 2:
Organize the revolving debt from smallest to largest.

Step 3:
Set all the minimum payments up as automatic withdrawals.

DEBT SNOWBALL WORKSHEET

(Smallest To Largest)	Balance	Monthly Payment	Snowball Payment	New Balance	Payoff Date
Total					

Step 4:

Based on your monthly budget, put all leftover money towards paying off the smallest account.

Step 5:

Use the same strategy for each revolving debt or credit card.

The third strategy you can do to make sure to optimize your utilization rate, is to request credit limit increases. Every six to nine months, you can be eligible for your creditors to increase the limit on the credit available to you. Whether or not you are granted the credit limit increase is dependent on the credit utilization and payment history in that period. If you manage your credit responsibility, you will be given financing offers from other credit card companies and the cards you have will give you more credit as well. Practice good credit habits on all your credit items and this option will be available to you to great effect.

Length of Credit

Length of credit is a key element of credit scoring which is strengthened by time. Credit is based on a relationship. A creditor entrusts you with money. How you pay it back will impact that relationship positively. If payments are made on time and balances are kept low, then a positive relationship is created. If payments are missed or untimely or credit is overused, this creates a negative relationship. The longer the relationship is with the creditor, the better it is for you if you are in good standing.

For example, if somebody has been able to make all their payments on time for a year, compared to somebody who has made their payments on time for 10 years, the person with the ten-year history of consistency would have earned more trust and more financing power over time.

Since the length of time an account has been opened can help credit scores increase, closing an account can cause a score to drop. Keeping a credit line open allows the positive credit history to report monthly. Additionally, if the card is paid off, the utilization will have an ongoing positive impact on the score every month. The impact of this can be seen when a new revolving account is added. If there are credit cards that have been established for years, the average age of the credit will drop, and the FICO score could drop as well.

Credit Mix

Credit cards are the easiest type of credit to attain. Many people develop a credit card dependency. Using varied forms of credit shows a level of responsibility and purpose in the pursuit of credit. Credit mix isn't the biggest piece of the pie, but if you use it the right way, that could be the difference between your credit being a 700 and a 720.

New Credit

Steve was fed up. He was tired of his rent going up and his living condition getting worse. He told me he made good money and saved much of it yet would not be able to buy a house because he knew his credit was bad. He was financially devastated during the Great Recession of 2008 and all the credit cards he had went into collections. He had not established credit since.

To Steve's delight, when he checked his credit, he saw how all the collection accounts were no longer on his credit, and he effectively had a clean slate. His goal to buy a house "someday" turned into buying a house within six months. By getting a secured credit card and getting approved for a secured savings account, he now had credit. The new credit he established had his credit score go into the high 600s in less than three months. New credit is weighed against the credit that is on a credit profile. If an account is established for years, the new credit can have a negative impact as it will cause the average length of credit history to decrease. On the other hand, if new credit is added to a new or renewed credit profile, it can cause the credit score to increase rapidly. When new credit is the only story being told on a credit report, how it is managed from the start is very important.

Steve was able to meet the credit score requirement for a mortgage in a short period of time and his new credit helped him get into a new house. When looking to buy a home, a feature of new credit to consider is inquiries. Whenever you apply for credit, the "inquiry" is reported on a credit report. When a consumer is actively looking for credit and submitting multiple applications, there will be a negative impact to the credit score. The higher the rate of credit requested the more significant the impact is to the score. When applying for a mortgage, or automobile financing, the credit bureaus do not penalize inquiries as severely. This is because consumers are encouraged to shop for the most favorable financing options.

Having these five credit factors work for you will help you take advantage of points that are currently not benefiting your credit and having them benefit you.

Budgeting

A budget is a detailed outline of all your income and expenses (down to the penny) for a given period. Setting goals and clearly defining your actions to meet these goals is budgeting. Budgeting helps you to prioritize your spending based on what you say you want for your life. By doing this you will be able to manage money to eliminate wasteful spending habits, and channel income in the right directions to achieve financial goals. According to a survey done by Forbes Magazine, just 37% of Americans have enough savings to pay for a $500 or $1,000 emergency. The Pew Charitable Trust also reports that one in three American families have no savings at all. Budgeting decreases surprises and stress levels because knowing exactly where money is being spent offers financial clarity.

Budgeting will help you to realize your money goals with a few simple approaches you can use as a daily routine. Like any other great achievement, discipline is required. Like most things, there are numerous ways to skin a cat, and budgeting is no different. Based on your preference, there are several strategies you may take to get to your personal finance goals in the style that works best for you.

A great place to start is by getting your bank statements, tax returns, and credit report together. With these key documents, the numbers will reveal themselves. If you thought you were on your way, confirmation is shown in these documents. If not, you get the opportunity to recalibrate your current habits and structure a plan that will support your goals. The following information shows a few budgeting techniques you can start today.

MONTHLY BUDGET AND GOALS

	Due Date	Budget Amount	Actual Amount	Difference	Budget Percentage	Actual Percentage
Income						
Must Haves						
Savings / Investing / Lifestyle						
Wants						
Totals						
Total Incomes						
Must Haves						
Savings						
Wants						
Total Outgoing						
Total Leftover						

This powerful and popular tool sets you on track to build your budget by giving a guideline for your needs, wants, and savings. According to this method Championed by Senator Elizabeth Warren, 50% of your income should be assigned to needs, 30% to wants, and 20% to savings. This is a very conservative model that asks you to save a lot of your income, but the long-term gains can be immense.

Needs

Needs include housing payments, car payments, groceries, insurance, health care, minimum debt payment, and utilities. Some things like your coffee habit or getting a brand-new car may feel like needs, but if they are not essential to making life work, they don't go into this category. Needs are expenses which are vital for survival.

When looking at this 50/30/20 ratio for income, many people say, "there's no way possible all of my needs fit into 50% of my income." It's okay because most people don't start going to the gym with six pack abs. They work and work until they get their desired body. Here, people get to work towards a financial life that puts them back in the driver's seat of their finances. When you are starting out don't expect for everything to be a perfect fit. The first step is to set the 50/30/20 ratio as your financial goal. From there set goals to cut costs in the areas you can control to climb closer and closer to financial wellness.

Our needs, wants, and savings will change over time. Maybe an emergency caused you to go into debt at some point in your life. Once you find level footing and can pay off that debt, the amount you need to pay towards your credit card minimum payments will go down. If you have a car loan and pay it off, your budget for needs will be reduced as well. Target bills that are in the need section of your budget and work to eliminate them while resisting the temptation to add to your expenses. In time, the 50% of your income required for this system will become more of a reality.

Wants

Your wants can be summed up into all those things that make life more comfortable and enjoyable. Wants can account for the difference between an economy car, which can be a need, and a luxury vehicle, which may be a want. It also includes the difference between dinner and going out to eat. All your entertainment from your Netflix to going out with friends are accounted for here. Clothes are a necessity. If you don't believe me, go to work without them! Those designer shoes, fancy handbags, and name brand clothes do cross the line from a need to a want. Comfort and necessity are not the same. While you may want to live your best life with the best the world has to offer, your desires come after taking care of the basics.

A client of mine named Nicole was committed to having a steak for dinner with octopus for her appetizer every Friday after a long week at work. It was her treat to herself for being dedicated and showing restraint for not losing it with the people at her job. When I asked her if she would be willing to cut out this expense to pay down her debt, she said, "I work hard and feel like I deserve to be able to treat myself to dinner." It is very important to reward yourself for the work you do at work and home, but at what cost?

My client eventually saw where her $65 meal was costing her more than just $3,380 for the year. It was costing her interest on credit card debt she could be eliminating, and it was costing her the money she could be saving for a down payment on her house. Nicole was on track to spend $3,380 in one year for one fancy dinner a week, not to mention her other meals. To her that time to decompress with a fine meal meant so much—yet, did she have other goals which meant more? Nicole decided she loved her Friday date nights with herself. She also chose to be more responsible with her finances. She found a restaurant that gave her a nice dining experience for less than half the price. This is an example of finding a win/win where she was able to get what she wanted now and was able to save for what she wanted most. A home to call her own. The last 20% of this budgeting equation is savings. I'll come back to this shortly.

Zero-Based Budget

What you measure you can manage. With a zero-based budget, you are tracking every dollar and every expense. The purpose here is to calculate every dollar going to expenses and at the same time also being intentional about every dollar left over. Is your extra money going to debt, savings, or some other place? Either way, this method audits your monthly flow to the penny. This way, budgeters can plan how long debt will be paid off, how long before you can get the down payment for that house, and any other financial goals you have. This is a more tedious method of budgeting but imagine if your GPS dropped you off in the general area you are looking to go to. Precision matters and the zero-based budget ensures it.

This method of money management ensures that if you bring in $4,000 a month, $4,000 a month goes where it is supposed to. Like any other personal finance tool, you're going to take care of your housing expenses, car, and other needs and then proceed to pay for your debts, wants, and savings. There are other methods that allow for a surplus, like the envelope method you will learn about shortly. With this method, the zero-based budgeting isn't a success until every dollar is accurately applied to its task. You will have to hold yourself accountable and diligently track your money. This can feel like a job that restricts you, but it's giving you the freedom to work towards any goal you want to go after.

Savings and Debt

You might wonder, does it make sense to save money while you are in debt? According to the FDIC, the average savings account in the United States yields 0.04% interest. Compare this to an average interest rate of 14.85% for existing credit card accounts. Saving while in debt is like throwing water out of a sinking ship using a cup. After establishing an emergency fund for $1,000, eliminating debt is the next step to financial wellness. Savings and debt are put into the same category because the money going to debt today will be going to savings once the debt is gone.

The 20% recommended for savings in this 50/30/20 plan mentioned above, is one that is a huge stretch for many. Any retirement plans are included into the saving totals. To make this strategy most effective, maximizing pre-tax savings plans will make a portion of savings automated.

There is no expectation for anyone to be at the 50/30/20 rule percentages when you start. With time, saving 20% of your income will get closer and closer to reality. These are ideal budgeting ratios as you commit to eliminating debt, spending intentionally, and saving. Develop these skills and watch them transform your life. Having this strategy as the basis of your finances, will allow you to achieve financial freedom exponentially faster than someone who does not have a plan.

As you break down your income based on this method of budgeting, don't be discouraged if you are not in alignment with this strategy now. For many, the idea of having a plan for money is a new concept. Be patient and forgive yourself if this doesn't become your lifestyle right away. With this system, the 20% that you are saving with every paycheck will have a huge compounding effect which will play a big part in how your financial future plays out.

The Envelope Method

One of the more popular and old school styles of budgeting is the envelope method. My grandmother used to always have different envelopes with cash for different purposes. She had one envelope for gas, one for groceries, and others I never thought to ask about. One envelope was money from her tenants. If she would have told me what she was doing, she could've saved me so much of the money I blew in my 20's.

Granny was practicing an age-old method that helped her to budget cash and manage money like a pro. One of the key reasons the "Envelope Method" works so well is that it is a tangible way to manage your money. With this strategy, you mark envelopes for your monthly expenses. The envelopes can separate money into categories like, your groceries, entertainment, clothing, and restaurants. This is a great way to manage variable and leisure expenses. With the advances of online banking, instead of using physical envelopes with cash, you can separate accounts for needs, wants, and savings so you may effectively track your money when you want. This is one of the best ways to give each dollar an assignment.

A challenge to finding success with the envelope budgeting method is technology. We have transitioned into an electronic society. Banking, budgeting, and even shopping is done online. Having to go to the bank or the ATM makes this a cumbersome task. With our busy lives, adding another errand can make this a less appealing option for your financial management. Fortunately, there are online tools that allow you to use the Envelope Method from the comfort of your mobile device.

Celebrate Good Times

Getting your envelope right for the month is a big deal! When you start out, you may experience growing pains but when you get to the point where you have money left in your envelope, you've won! Celebrate your success. If you can do this in one area of your finances, think about what is possible when you are consistent in managing all your money for the month. We're talking about a shift that can have implications of long-term financial growth and peace. That deserves your acknowledgement and praise. Make sure your celebrations do not undermine the work you've already done. What money is left over, use towards your savings or towards paying off debt and your financial dreams will find you faster.

Take stock of your financial situation. How much do you own and how much do you owe? Many of us may feel as if we know what our financial status is, yet, we are assuming and not sure of our financial standing. Do you have financial goals? What is the timeline for you to accomplish them and how far along are you? Just the idea of having to look in the mirror and accept the reality of one's financial position is enough to cause stress and panic for some. When you consider the social security income that your grandparents were able to live from is less than guaranteed for any generation after them, are you being irresponsible with your lives to not face these facts head on? That's what a budget allows you to do. Once it's on paper, you are at least clear as to your starting position.

Blueprint 2

The Student Loan Dilemma
Christian and Ayana

My sister Ayana is in her early 30s, but it feels like she's been in school for 40 years. Needless to say, she ended up with a few student loans. She and her husband Christian were planning to buy for about a year, yet they kept on bumping into the same issue. The student loan debt was throwing off the debt-to-income ratio. Christian and Ayana are smart, or maybe they had a good advisor, yet they decided they were going to do everything possible to get the home loan done in just one of their names.

The plan was to buy the first house in Ayana's name and then the second one in Christian's name when they found a good deal. Everything was going according to plan except that this student loan issue kept coming up. What I advised Ayana to do was to get into a student loan repayment plan. The benefit for an educator like Ayana is that she was able to sign up for the Public Service Loan Forgiveness program simultaneously.

What it did for her was instead of having a percentage of her full student loan balance being used, she was able to get a loan payment which was significantly lower than her standard payment.

Once a payment plan is agreed upon with a student loan servicer, a lender must use the payment amount in the DTI (Debt-to-Income ratio). This is true even if the payment plan amount is $1.

Finally, Ayana and Christian were able to bypass the student loan issue. They were given a mortgage pre-approval letter and started the process of looking for their new home. They went out looking for houses on almost a daily basis. They made offer after offer and kept on getting close, but they just missed out for one reason or the next.

After making over 30 offers, they got an offer accepted and closed on their home. Ayana said, "watching my son run around in his backyard made it all worth it." She and Christian bought a home with "potential." That's code for ugly and tacky in this case. If you don't believe me, just ask the life-sized stuffed bear that was in the living room when they bought it. Everything was dated but being in a seller's market, they still had to pay close to the asking price.

Months on, they have gotten rid of the giant bear, and renovated the house. Now it is truly a beautiful home. They had the vision to see how what they were buying was not the finished article. It was most important for them to get into a house and gradually make it a home. The repairs they did have helped the home to build equity and generate income.

"A few months ago, we were renting out a part of our house, now we are renting out the first floor of our house as two apartments. Our tenants are paying our mortgage for us instead of us paying a mortgage for a landlord. Based on what people are paying for rent, you see the biggest difference isn't the monthly payment but the down payment," Ayana stated. "We needed good credit to rent so we figured we had to find a way to stop renting and start owning."

I asked her, how did you manage to get the down payment for your house? She said, "we saved like we've never saved before. We did it and we know anyone can do it if they put their minds to it."

"What was the hardest part of the process for you?"

"Writing the check for the down payment and closing cost had me a little uptight. My husband reminded me we were not spending money; we were investing it."

"Now that you bought your first home, what is possible?"

"Things are going so great with this house in such a short period of time that we're already looking for our second house. All our goals are on a higher level now. Our home is a springboard to the wealth we want to create for our family."

"What message would you give to people who had the same issues you faced?"

"Save like your life depends on it. It's the biggest difference between being a tenant and having tenants pay your mortgage. My husband and I are so motivated to change our world as we know it, because we did this even when we were being told no. We ended up finding a house that allowed us to build equity quickly by doing repairs. With what we've learned, we're looking to do even better on our next house," Ayana said.

Blueprint for Buying Despite Student Loan Debt

1. Go to www.nlsds.ed.gov to get the full details of your total federal student loan debt.
2. Request a repayment plan with the lowest monthly payment.
3. Enroll in the Loan Rehabilitation program if your loan is in default.
4. Apply for Public Service Loan Forgiveness if eligible.
5. Save for your home like your life depends on it.

CHAPTER 3

Unlocking Your Home Team

There are many professionals who are involved in the process of you closing on your home. To have to go through the journey by yourself can be intimidating. That's why it's important to have a team to help you navigate the course. With so many moving parts, where do you start?

As a buyer, you can do all of this by yourself, which has its benefits and disadvantages. If you are looking to buy a house not listed with a Realtor, you can have an opportunity to negotiate a better price.

When properties are on the Multiple Listing Service or MLS, the price is increased because it will have more exposure to buyers. The MLS is a marketplace where Realtors post all the "listed" properties in a particular area. As a property hits the MLS, all the Realtors with access to the MLS can see them and present them to the buyers they are working with.

Without all those eyes on a property, a buyer won't have as much competition for a house. In the same vein, the home seller won't be able to access as many buyers. The disadvantage as a buyer is not having the support of an area expert who can find the home with the specific details the buyer is looking for. The trade-off can be a big one. In a competitive market, not having a Realtor in your corner can make it harder to find the right home. They are the ones with their finger on the pulse of the market. What areas are hot, which are not, what details will make a home sell faster, and how much you should offer to get your offer accepted, are all things a Realtor can help with.

As vital as a Realtor is to you finding your home, the Realtor is not the first step on this path. Before a Realtor does their work with a buyer, the buyer must be "pre-approved." The teammate who does this is your lender. Your lender can be a banker or a broker.

Choose Your Lender

The difference between a banker and a broker is that a banker is a direct lender, and a broker works with many banks to get the best deal. When getting a traditional loan program like a FHA or a Conventional mortgage, the difference between the two are not significant. A broker's real value comes with non-traditional loan programs such as bank statement loans or loans for self-employed borrowers.

Lenders take clients through an application to determine if they meet the credit requirements, debt-to-income ratios, and have the resources to be able to close. When a buyer gets through this step successfully, they will receive a "pre-approval."

With a pre-approval letter in hand, a borrower can start working with a real estate agent on their home search. After the initial application, a lender will be waiting for you to find the house, get your offer accepted, and get into contract. Once the lender receives the contract from the real estate agent, they will process your loan application to get you the funding you need to close.

LENDER INTERVIEW QUESTIONS

1. Are you licensed by the state?

2. Whom do you represent (e.g., a bank, broker, finance company)?

3. What are your loan programs?

4. What is the pare rate (the actual rate for a particular loan) for a 30-year fixed loan.

5. Can you estimate and explain your fees?

6. Are you going to hold this loan or sell it?

7. How long have you been working as a mortgage professional?

8. Do you have experience with borrowers in a similar situation to me?

9. What is the interest rate you are offering, and how did you arrive at it?

10. How do I know this is the best rate?

11. How will the rate change over the life of the loan?

12. If an adjustable-rate mortgage (ARM), what is the worst-case scenario I could face when the rate resets?

13. Could you estimate closing costs for my loan?

14. Can you explain an annual percentage rates (APR), and what is it for this loan.

15. What am I paying in points?

16. What are my monthly payments?

17. Do I need to pay private mortgage insurance (PMI)?

18. Are there any prepayment penalties on this loan?

19. Here's my timeline. Are you certain you can get this done in time for closing?

Lender Questions

Here are some questions to ask your lender to see if they are the right one to handle the financing for your home.

The financing for your home is your lifeline to this entire process. Take the time to choose the mortgage professional you feel confident and comfortable with. When you get pre-approved for a mortgage, your banker will need to obtain your credit report. When they do, you will have an inquiry on your credit report. While credit inquiries can have a negative impact on credit scores, only one inquiry will impact the score during a 14-30-day window. This is because the latest FICO credit scoring model gives consumers an opportunity to shop for the best rate and terms on a mortgage without being penalized.

With the ability to interview up to three mortgage bankers, you can be assured to get the best options available for you. To find the professionals to work with, seek the recommendation of a real estate agent, real estate professional, or a family member or friend who has recently gotten a mortgage. From there, go through the interview questions and decide which mortgage professional will give you the best deal.

During the interview process, your mortgage professional will ask for documentation to prove how much income can be used for the debt-to-income ratios. It will feel like they are invading every inch of your financial privacy, but just like a doctor, let them do their job to give you the right diagnosis. How much of a loan you qualify for, as well as how low of an interest rate you are qualified for, are determined by these documents.

Here is a checklist of the required documentation:

- One month of your most recent pay stubs
- W-2 tax forms for the last 2 years
- Personal tax returns for the last 2 years (all schedules)
- A copy of your driver's license and social security card

What comes next is: Congratulations! YOU'RE PRE-APPROVED!

Now that you are pre-approved, you have a license to shop! To help you get access to more properties and options you can hire a real estate agent.

Choosing the Right Real Estate Agent

If you call a Realtor a real estate agent, they will be quick to correct you. While they perform the same job, there is a distinction between them. First let me tell you about what that job is.

A real estate agent is a real estate professional who helps clients with the buying and selling of their properties. They have been licensed to sell real estate by successfully completing a course and passing a national and state exam. They can be licensed to do real estate in as many regions as they go through the licensing process for. Real estate agents generally focus in one region and can specialize in residential or commercial properties.

Some agents choose to pursue a niche as a listing agent, a buyer's agent, or a rental agent.

Listing Agent

Listing agents focus on serving homeowners who want to sell their property. These agents usually are more experienced and have been able to build a clientele base who trust them. Their expert understanding of what a house can sell for and what can be done to give a seller the best chance of getting the best price is part of what they offer you. A good listing agent can be a strong negotiator as they are tasked with reviewing the offers made on a property they have listed. They will attempt to drive the price as high as possible while keeping the buyers interested. They must be able to navigate the differences between negotiating in a buyers and a sellers' market to get their client the best result regardless of the time they chose to sell.

Buyer's Agent

A buyer's agent serves aspiring home buyers to help them find homes the buyers want. They are dream makers. They must find the balance between everything a buyer wants and what a buyer can afford. Often buyers have eyes that are richer than their wallets, so a good buyer's agent must temper expectations. Their job is to keep a buyer on a realistic track for what they can afford and what the market is offering.

Rental Agents

Rental agents work with the rental market to have properties listed for rent and to help renters find a place to rent. Rental agents are usually new agents who are learning their target area's real estate market. Since rental transactions close quickly and are always going on, it gives less experienced agents a chance to do business without having to wait for the larger and longer deals to close.

A real estate agent can operate in any of these capacities on a deal-by-deal basis. An agent can be the listing agent for one deal, the buyer's agent for another deal, or both on another. They can even do apartments on the side. A real estate agency commission is split into two parts. There is the listing commission and the sales commission. If the real estate fee is 4% of the sale, then the listing agency gets paid 2% and the selling agency gets paid a 2% commission. If the listing agent also sells the property, they receive the entire 4% fee.

A Realtor is a real estate agent who is an active member of the National Association of Realtors. To become a member, they must have a valid real estate license and a clean professional conduct record. They are held to a different standard because they agree to uphold The Code of Ethics in dealing with their clients, other Realtors, and the public. The Code of Ethics is an enforceable set of ethical guidelines which are firmly upheld by the Board of Realtors.

This distinction makes a Realtor more accountable. They promise to ethically perform their duties to their clients and their industry. A real estate agent can still be great at what they do. While each professional you consider working with should be interviewed and vetted, the title of Realtor should be weighed positively in your consideration.

A real estate agent is often the first point of contact for home buyers. Though getting pre-approved by a mortgage lender is the first official step, the real estate agent is the quarterback of the whole process. They can introduce you to your lender, your inspector, and everyone else who plays a part in your home purchase.

Their value cannot be overstated. Before you find your home, they will help your vision unfold by giving recommendations on homes, neighborhoods, and finishing styles based on what is important to you and your budget. You may have one type of property in your mind, yet after speaking with your Realtor, you may discover more options available to you in an area you didn't expect.

A good Realtor will be your negotiator, your confidant, motivator, and counselor. They can even play the role of chauffeur on those house hunting weekends! With the amount of time you will spend with your Realtor, taking the time to get to choose the right one is one of the most important things you can do during the process.

There are some real estate agents who are knowledgeable but may put their desire to make a commission in front of your needs. Others may only be part-time and not be able to give you the attention you will need. Some Realtors just may not be the kind of person you want to spend weekends house hunting with.

To make your selection process more targeted, use the following worksheet.

WHICH REAL ESTATE AGENCY TO USE

Instructions: Use this worksheet to compare which real estate agent and agency is best for you.

Write Names Of Agency, Contact Person, And Phone Number.	A.	What did they say? Codes
	B.	Y = Yes
	C.	N = No
	D.	? = Don't know
	E.	- = Not applicable

	Questions to Ask	Response Columns				
		A	B	C	D	E
1	How long has the agency been in business? The Realtor? Over three years is good.					
2	Does the agency advertise? Where? How often?					
3	Are you comfortable with the agent?					
4	Does the agent seem to know the neighborhoods you are interested in?					
5	Can the agent answer questions about taxes, school districts, square feet, etc.?					
6	Is the agent good at returning your calls quickly?					
7	Is the agent comfortable getting answers they don't know for you quickly?					
8	Does the agent seem to be easy to work with and like what they are doing?					
9	Does the agent get back to you with answers to questions that he or she did not know initially?					
10	What is your trust level with the agent? Agency?					
11	Does the agent help educate you about what is good and what needs work?					
12	Does the agent seem to respect you and your wishes?					
13	Does the agent have listings in the price range you want?					
14	Is the agent good with helping you troubleshoot and problem solve, as needed?					

Now that you have the captain of your team, you can rest assured knowing that an expert is going to be assembling the rest of the deal making team. You cannot imagine how many wheels are moving while you're waiting to close. It's like looking at the watch and seeing the hands move but you don't see the gears in the back doing all the work.

Your Realtor is the one conducting the orchestra. The people they would recommend for the inspection are usually people that they've worked with and trust. Don't forget all this work your agent does is in vain unless the deal is closed. They will generally only refer professionals they have closed with before. They won't risk your home search, and their livelihood, on people they are not sure about.

Following are some of the other key players and what they do.

Inspector

An inspector evaluates a property once you have it under contract. They thoroughly inspect the property to assure it is structurally sound and in compliance with construction regulations. They include their findings in a report which will help a buyer determine if there are any issues with the house. In the event the inspector finds significant damage in the property the buyer can decide to walk away from the property and get their deposit back. They can also use the findings in the inspector's report to renegotiate the deal. When purchasing a home, most contracts have a provision that gives the buyer an "inspection period" which is the time frame they are given to continue with the deal or walk away without losing their deposit. The inspection period can be used as a leverage point when submitting an offer. If a buyer offers a shorter inspection period, it will be considered a positive sign for the seller.

Appraiser

The property appraiser evaluates the property to assess the value it holds in the current market. Appraisers look at the property condition, the neighborhood, and comparable sales to determine how much the property is worth. The appraisal is used by the bank to assess how much they can lend to a borrower. If a property is being sold for $400,000 yet the appraisal only came in for $360,000, the bank would base the loans they are offering on the appraised value rather than the sales price.

Title Company

The title company is responsible for examining and insuring title claims for real estate. They verify ownership of property and determine the valid owner through a thorough analysis of property records in a title search. The title company usually does an abstract of the title. The title abstract determines the legal owner of the property; details any mortgages, liens, judgments, or unpaid taxes outstanding on the property; and reveals any existing restrictions, easements, or leases that effect the property. After completing the abstract, the company will issue a title opinion letter. This will lay out all the things that should be done and any problems that should be fixed before a purchaser can receive a good title.

Closing Attorney

A bank real estate attorney prepares and reviews all the documents that are signed at a closing for a real estate purchase. The attorney would also be at the closing on behalf of the bank. In some states, a title company can assume these responsibilities. They can also be instrumental in handling any disputes between the buyer and seller at closing. In states like New York and New Jersey, the buyer must hire an attorney to represent them in a purchase or a refinance. The attorney's role is to ensure the transfer is legal, binding, and in the best interests of the client.

There are even more professionals who are involved with the home buying process, but these are the most prominent ones who will have the ability to make or break your deal. Scary, isn't it? Only a few can make the deal, but there's a whole list of those who can break your deal.

Property Insurance

The property insurance agent provides a homeowner's insurance policy prior to the purchase being finalized. For a bank to finance a property, they require adequate property insurance.

This emphasizes how important it is to get a great captain who is not going to take chances with your goals.

This can be intimidating. Here's the secret:

Do all the research you can do by looking at online reviews and conducting thorough interviews, then let go and let the real estate agent do their thing. You are the boss, so you will have to manage the process, but once you've done all you can do, trust that you chose the right person.

When you take the time upfront to interview and vet the people you will spend the better part of months working with, you will know that they have your back. If you don't feel like you can relax while they are at the wheel, either you must check yourself—or if your Realtor or banker is slipping—let them slide right out of your business.

You are the boss! Let me say this again. Even though you are the least experienced, least knowledgeable person in this equation, nobody gets paid until you're happy. Well, almost nobody. The inspector and the appraiser get off easy because they get paid up front. Everyone else must earn your business throughout the process.

Have you ever had an assignment to complete at work and your manager is on your back asking you all the questions? Don't be like that. Give the people you put in place to get the job done room to maneuver but get regular updates to make sure everything you are required to do is communicated to you and gets done.

Blueprint 3

Right House, Wrong Lender
Kevin and Shantae

Kevin and Shantae were high school sweethearts. They got married and had a beautiful daughter. Living in New York however, the prices made it hard to buy a house. They rented and were comfortable, until their family was getting ready to grow. When I asked Kevin what their motivation was, he said, "we needed space. We had one child and one on the way. It was like the rent was increasing while the space was shrinking. It was time to try and see if we could make it work."

He and Shantae got to work to make this homeowner dream a reality. They found a nice house close to the family. The offer got accepted and they were going through the process of getting their mortgage. However, they noticed their lender kept on asking them for the same paperwork. When they submitted the most recent pay stub, they would get a request a week later for the same thing. This was going on for weeks. Luckily, they bought in a buyer's market, so the seller was not stressing them to close. Their stress was an internal stress. Literally!

Their unborn son was getting bigger and bigger by the week, and it felt like they were in a race against time to close. After getting a call from the lender with him requesting the same documents again, Shantae finally said, "if you can't close this in a week, don't call me, we'll find somebody else." Miraculously his next call was to tell them the loan was "Cleared to Close."

They were able to close with time to set up the baby's room just right. I asked Kevin, "What is it like to be a homeowner compared to a tenant?" He said, "I can walk around my house however I want, and nobody can't tell me anything!" He laughed with an empowered assurance. "My mindset is totally different. Everything you do in the house is for you and for yours. It's a way better feeling than seeing that something isn't working and waiting for a landlord to fix it because now I'm fixing it for my family and me."

I continued by asking him, "what is the best part about being a homeowner?"

He responded, "Setting the trend for my children to see. Now it's expected for them to be homeowners too one day."

I asked, "What's your favorite part of your house?"

"My man cave!" He responded with no hesitation. "It took me five years to be able to set it up the way that I want it, but now it's my favorite place and the best part of the house."

Shantae said, "I love to sit on the chair swing in the backyard, watch the kids play and do things like roast smores and just chill. It's simple but it means everything to me."

Kevin interjected and said, "I love looking at the manicured lawn and just enjoying our house. My homeowner skills got crazy! I can fix most things around the house, and I have a nice garden. I grow my tomatoes, peppers, mint, and marijuana. I never thought I'd be a gardener!"

When I asked, "Have you been able to build equity?" Shantae had a resounding answer. "In 6 years, we've built over 6 figures in equity. We can dream bigger and make bigger plans for our family. It's a whole new world of options for us now!"

Kevin and Shantae are another example of all the blessings homeownership has in store for those who commit to making it happen at any cost.

Blueprint for Finding the Right Real Estate Pros

1. As the buyer, know that you are the boss and act as such.
2. Interview more than one Realtor and lender and keep the 2nd choice as a backup.
3. Cooperate with your real estate professionals to help them do their jobs efficiently.
4. Discuss your communication preferences with the professionals you work with.
5. Be willing to switch your lender or Realtor if they do not meet your needs (delayed paperwork, high fees, and poor communication are some common reasons to do so).

CHAPTER 4

Unlocking Home Loans

My sophomore year of college was a drag. I didn't want to be at Nassau Community College. I went to Albany State University in my freshman year and got in one little fight and my mom got scared. She kept me home and I went to the local community college. I was working at Delia's, a teeny-bopper clothing store and didn't have a next move. There was a class that met on Fridays and there was this one guy who always came to class talking about the money he made that week.

One week it was $600, then $800, and then $750. Each week was more than I was making in a month. I don't know if I was more annoyed or intrigued by his constant claims, but I had to know what he did. I asked him and he said, "I do mortgages. You should come down and check it out." I didn't even know what a mortgage was, but I wanted to find out. I went on an interview, and it changed my world forever. I learned about mortgage financing, real estate, credit, sales, and became an expert in the home buying process.

A mortgage is a loan taken out against the value of a property. The lower the percentage of the property value borrowed, the lower the risk. Lenders offer financing based on criteria which determines the level of risk. They look at credit, debt-to-income ratios, and equity (down payment included). A borrower applying for a loan 65% of the value of a property is less of a risk than a borrower applying for a loan 95% of the value of the property. A borrower with a 740 FICO score is less of a risk than a borrower with a 580 FICO score. These factors impact if money will be borrowed, how much money is borrowed, and the interest rate.

Getting a mortgage is a process with many moving parts. It requires borrowers to be able to prove they can maintain payments on a home by looking at how much of a mortgage they can afford. How much a borrower can afford is based on how much income they have in relation to their debt. This is called the debt-to-income ratio. Along with credit, and how much is being put down on a property, debt-to-income ratios determine if you can buy a house and what the loan amount can be.

Pre-qualification vs. Pre-approval

Most real estate professionals only get paid when you close. Therefore, Realtors need to focus their energy on people who have the desire and capacity to buy a home. When working with a buyer, they require proof the buyer has been deemed ready to buy by a lender. There are generally two paths taken to start the process. Buyers are pre-qualified or pre-approved. The difference is a pre-qualification is based on a preliminary verification of information required by a lender to help the buyer get a loan. This could be done verbally, or through a light documentation review.

The reason someone would get a pre-qualification is because it can be done quickly without the buyer having to produce a litany of documents. As a result, a pre-qualification letter does not hold much weight. In a competitive market, a seller is not likely to accept an offer from a buyer who can only produce a pre-qualification letter. Instead, they would prefer to work with a buyer who has been thoroughly pre-approved.

A pre-approval goes through the same process needed to approve a borrower for a mortgage. The buyer would do a credit check, submit their income documents for the last two years, and provide the source of their down payment. The only difference between a pre-approval and an approval from an underwriter is there would be no contract or appraisal submitted so the purchase price and the home value would be speculative. Every other piece of the equation would be reviewed and considered in determining the amount of the pre-approval.

You want to give yourself the best chance to get the best opportunities for you and your family. Submitting an offer with a pre-qualification is like using a cart that has the messed-up wheels at the grocery store. You won't get anywhere. Take the extra step to collect your required documents to submit to your lender and get a pre-approval letter. If your offer is accepted, you'll be much further along in your loan acquisition process, and sellers will take you more seriously.

Mortgage Interview Questions

You can expect to be asked the following questions, when getting interviewed to get pre-approved.

Unlocking Home Loans

Questions to complete	Applicant 1	Applicant 2
Name		
Address		
Social Security Number		
Date of Birth		
Current Employer		
Address		
Phone		
Position		
Years Employed		
Salary		
Highest Purchase Price		
Taxes for intended property		
Intended Down Payment		
Currently Rent or Own		
Current Monthly Mortgage or Rent		

Debt-to-Income (DTI)

Many people approach homeownership like they approach a buffet. Their desire is bigger than their appetite. Sure, everyone wants to have the picture-perfect home in a gated community with a walk-in closet, but that's not always an option. Especially not for people buying their first home. Once you've established the needs and wants for buying a home, you can see how much of that is available to you based on income, down payment, and the prices in the desired area. Keep in mind, where you start doesn't have to be where you end. A "starter home" can be just that. Where you start. With time and increases in income, more options and opportunities will become available. Get started with what you have.

Income is the part of the home buying process that is the least flexible. Lenders look at the last two years of income. Unlike credit that can experience a boost in a short period of time, your income from the last two years is what it is. To determine how much income goes into the debt-to-income ratio, banks most commonly use pay stubs, W-2s, and the Schedule 1040 on the tax return. There are caveats and exceptions to the rule, but in general this is the most common way to establish the "Gross Monthly Income."

22222	Void ☐	a Employee's social security number 123-45-6789	For Official Use Only ▶ OMB No. 1545-0008		
b Employer identification number (EIN) 12-1234567			1 Wages, tips, other compensation $50,000	2 Federal income tax withheld $5,098.50	
c Employer's name, address, and ZIP code Company ABC 123 Lee Road Columbus, OH 43004			3 Social security wages $50,000	4 Social security tax withheld $3,100.00	
			5 Medicare wages and tips $50,000	6 Medicare tax withheld $725.00	
			7 Social security tips	8 Allocated tips	
d Control number			9	10 Dependent care benefits	
e Employee's first name and initial Abby L.	Last name Smith		Suff 11 Nonqualified plans	12a See instructions for box 12	
f Employee's address and ZIP code 123 Sample Road Example City, OH 12345			13 Statutory employee / Retirement plan / Third-party sick pay	12b	
			14 Other	12c	
				12d	
15 State OH Employer's state ID number 12-3456789	16 State wages, tips, etc. $50,000	17 State income tax $1,320.43	18 Local wages, tips, etc. $50,000	19 Local income tax $1,250.00	20 Locality name Columbus

W-2 Wage and Tax Statement   2019

Form

Copy A For Social Security Administration — Send this entire page with Form W-3 to the Social Security Administration; photocopies are not acceptable.

Do Not Cut, Fold, or Staple Forms on This Page

Department of the Treasury—Internal Revenue Service

For Privacy Act and Paperwork Reduction Act Notice, see the separate instructions.

Cat. No. 10134D

For more information on how to properly fill out The W-2 Tax Statement to maximize you benefits, visit www.irs.gov/forms-pubs/about-form-w-2

Using the example of this W-2 the gross income from section "1" for the year is $50,000, which makes Gross Monthly Income $4,166.67 ($50,000 divided by 12).

Example:

If you pay $1,400 a month for your mortgage and another $100 a month for an auto loan and $200 a month for the rest of your debts, your monthly debt payments equal $1,700. ($1,400 + $100 + $200 = $1,700.) If your gross monthly income is $4,166.67, then your debt-to-income ratio is 41 percent. ($1,700 divided by $4,166.67 is 40.7 which is rounded up to 41%.)

Mortgage payments: $1,400

+

Auto loan: $100

+

Credit cards: $200

=

Gross monthly debt: $1,700

This is an oversimplified example of how income is determined. Seek professional advice for a more specific calculation.

The debt side of the DTI is determined by two separate equations. The first equation is the housing ratio or the front-end-DTI. This calculates how much of your income is going towards the mortgage payment as well as property taxes, property insurance, and mortgage insurance, if applicable. Lenders prefer borrowers who have a housing ratio of 28% or less. A mortgage banker would be able to calculate this ratio for you so you can start your home search with a specific target price to stay below. As an exercise to get an idea of what you can afford, you can try different price ranges to see what is realistic for you. To practice calculating the housing ratio, you can select a property online from Zillow or another real estate site, in the area you desire to live in.

Use the Home Affordability Worksheet to figure out how much home you can afford now!

When you know how much you can afford, it makes the home buying process more focused. You won't be wasting your time or a Realtor's time by looking into properties that are not in your budget. To get the most out of your home buying search, narrow down the price range to what you can afford and less.

Down Payment

One of the primary reasons for the Great Recession was the fall of the housing market. What made this possible was the high-risk loans became common practice. Homes were being purchased at 106%. Which means, not only were borrowers not required to put down a down payment, but they were also able to finance up to 6% of their closing costs. If one borrower put 10% on their property and the other got 106% financing, which do you think would do more to find a way to keep their house if they were facing a financial crisis?

While both would surely care about keeping the home, the borrower who put up 10% has much more to lose. Lenders have smartened up and now only grant loans to borrowers who are willing to put skin in the game. This decreases the rate of defaults on home loans and makes sure a borrower can handle the financial responsibilities of home ownership.

HOME AFFORDABILITY WORKSHEET

Monthly Mortgage Payment	
Monthly Property Tax Bill	
Monthly Insurance Premiums	
Total Monthly Principal, Interest, Taxes, and Insurance Costs (PITI)	
Gross Annual Household Income	
Gross Monthly Household Income	
Principal, Interest, Taxes, and Insurance Costs as a Percentage of Household Income	
Other Monthly Debt and Loan Payments	
Auto Loans	
Education Loans	
Credit Cards	
Personal Loans	
Other Debt Service	
Total Other Monthly Debt and Loan Payments	
Total PITI and Other Monthly Debt and Loan Payments	
Divide Total Other and Housing by Gross Income	
To qualify for a mortgage, your principal, interest, taxes, and insurance (PITI) should be less than 28% of gross household income, and PITI plus other monthly debt and loan payments should be less than 43% of gross household income.	

Where Is Your Down Payment?

Mortgage options change with time. At the time of this book being written, banks are offering loans with only 3.5% down. There are exceptions and programs that may be slightly lower and others that are slightly higher. Borrowers can use money from any account they own. If a borrower has a portion of the down payment in multiple accounts, they will have to provide two months of bank statements from each of these accounts.

Types of Accounts available to be use for a down payment.

- Checking
- Savings
- Traditional IRA
- Roth IRA
- Retirement Accounts
- 401k
- Life Insurance (Cash value)

Checking and saving accounts are the easiest accounts to use for a down payment. They are liquid and easily accessible. As a buyer, you would be permitted to close with a certified check from your bank the day of closing.

IRA's

An IRA or Individual Retirement Account is a popular financial tool. It allows people to compound their savings tax free or tax deferred. Since these accounts are supposed to be used for retirement, the IRS heavily penalizes any withdrawals made prior to the account holder turning 59 ½. One of the exceptions to this rule is that you can use funds from an IRA for a down payment of a home if you are a first-time home buyer. The IRS defines a first-time home buyer as someone who has not owned property in the last two years. You can also use an IRA to gift a down payment to an eligible child, grandchild, or a parent. A borrower is permitted to use up to $10,000 from your IRA as a first-time home buyer.

If you use your IRA to buy a home, the money should be repaid so the impact of compounding interest isn't lost on the down payment. The downside is you lose the compound interest on that amount toward your retirement, so all the time spent compounding that interest on your retirement is gone. You will also be required to pay income tax on the money withdrawn with certain accounts. Consult with your tax professional for advice on how and if you should use your IRA to buy a home.

401(k)

When taking out money from a 401(k) for the down payment of a property, there are a few key things you should know. Money taken out of a 401(k) for the purpose of buying a home will be a loan you must pay interest on. The good thing about it is the interest will be paid to your IRA. Most 401(k)'s offer five years to repay a loan. Speak with your financial advisor to see if this is the right option for you.

Life Insurance

Much like a 401(k), money taken out of a life insurance policy should be paid back with interest to the account. This way, you are allowed to have it help you attain a life goal and maintain a long-term account. Life insurance policies allow you to use the cash value of the account that has been accumulated from payments and dividends into the account over time.

The options given can help you to use money you might not have known you can use. Each of them comes with important financial nuances. Consult a financial advisor, tax professional, or a lawyer to be advised on your down payment options utilizing these types of accounts or others.

Mortgage Insurance (MI)

The more of a down payment by you, the more favorable lending terms are available to you. Lenders who offer FHA and Conventional Loans apply insurance on home loans that are purchased with a down payment less than 20% of the purchase price. FHA applies a mortgage insurance premium to protect the bank in the event of a borrower defaulting on loan payments.

A large down payment offers security to all parties involved in a home purchase. The seller and the lender feel secure because the buyer is putting a significant financial commitment into the deal. The borrower owns a larger percentage of the home. When a borrower cannot put down a larger down payment, the seller and the lender are taking more of a chance. To prevent losses due to borrower default, banks require borrowers to pay mortgage insurance.

For FHA Loans borrowers don't have to pay Private Mortgage Insurance (PMI), but they will have to pay an Up-Front Mortgage Insurance Premium (MIP) and an annual Mortgage Insurance Premium instead. Whether the down payment is 5% or 10% on an FHA Insured Loan, there will be the upfront and annual premiums charged. If there is a 10% down payment or more, the MIP will be removed after the loan is less than 80% of the original amount. For loans that are taken out with less than a 10% down payment, the MIP will be required for the life of the loan.

MIP has always been a feature of FHA Loans. However, the latest version of the FHA Loan makes MIP harder to remove. While 20% equity in a property used to be the only factor, now down payment amounts matter as much. Any FHA Loan that is taken out with a down payment less than 10% will have mortgage insurance for the life of the loan. If there is a down payment of 10% or more, a mortgage insurance premium will be charged until the loan is less than 80% of the appraised value of the house. Mortgage insurance is charged upfront at the closing and monthly as a premium. The UFMIP, or Up-Front Mortgage Insurance Premium is currently 1.75% of the base loan amount.

Down Payment Assistance

Education is a vital component of the home buying process. Often when I conduct home buying seminars there are attendees who believe they can't buy a home because they haven't saved 20% for a down payment on a home. Since 2002, there have been loan programs that have allowed buyers to close with 0%, 3.5%, or even 5% down. There were even programs giving the buyer a loan for 106% of the purchase price. Mortgage loans have not required 20% down for over 20 years. The significance of 20% down is the mortgage insurance factor.

Every time I hear someone say, "I don't have 20% to put down on a house," I think, "Where did they get that idea from, and how many people think like this?" This is an alarming limitation. For people who already faced an uphill battle to claim homeownership, the idea of saving such a massive amount of money could be the nail in the coffin of hope. For most Americans, a 20% down payment would be a bridge too far. For those who are stretching themselves to make this a reality, this could be an insurmountable barrier.

Fortunately, not only do home buyers not need 20% down, but there is a wealth of resources that help home buyers get the down payment through grants and government programs. They can help home buyers climb to the next step. Down payment assistance is accessible nationwide and is based on a few key factors.

Eligibility Factors for DPA

- Credit score
- Income
- Profession
- Household size
- Neighborhood

- Median household income of new neighbor-hood
- Length of time required to live in the home
- Complete an 8-hour class

How DPA Works

Down payment assistance (DPA) is a broad term used to describe programs offered by federal, state, county, or local government agencies, nonprofit organizations, and employers. These programs are offered in two forms:

- Grants that do not have to be repaid
- Second mortgage loans with varying payback or forgiveness solutions

Grants

Grants are gifts provided by an eligible third-party agency at the closing. These funds do not have to be paid back by the homeowner. Grants used for down payment assistance and closing costs do not incur a lien on the property nor will they be on the deed.

Second Mortgage

Most down payment assistance programs are given as a second mortgage. Some of these can be forgiven after the borrower has occupied the property for a specified period. Other second mortgages from down payment assistance programs must be paid off when refinancing or selling the property. Generally, there is little, or no, interest charged on these second mortgages.

There are over 2,000 down payment assistance programs across the country. The primary source for these programs is the Department of Housing and Urban Development or HUD. HUD participates in these programs for community development. The goal is to restore communities by offering incentives to first-time home buyers for purchasing homes in economically distressed neighborhoods. While the intention is to create a win-win by helping people who have limited funds and communities in need of TLC, buyers are not restricted to distressed neighborhoods.

If a buyer finds a home in a more desirable neighborhood, if their income qualifies for the home price, they could buy where they want with most DPA programs. With down payment assistance being limited by income and family size, it is more likely for a buyer to purchase in a community with a lower sales price.

DPA for Educators and First Responders

Traditional DPA programs focus on people who do not make too much money, for the sake of them being deemed eligible. There are other programs that are created to help the people who help people. Educators, police officers, firefighters, and Paramedics can get down payment assistance through a few different sources.

The Good Neighbor Next Door is an offering from HUD which gives these professionals options to purchase cheap homes with favorable financing options. These HUD homes are usually vacant and distressed, and in depressed communities. This is a great option for those who are eligible, but there is very little inventory available so it does not have the reach and impact it could.

Lenders are going to be the primary go-to source for options for down payment assistance and help with closing costs. They can give credits to close. They can also be affiliated with agencies who offer DPA programs. Whether the aim is to get traditional DPA or DPA for a public service career, starting with options from your lender will put you on the right track to get all you can to close.

Seller's Concession

Another option to help buyers with closing costs is a seller's concession. A seller's concession is when the seller gives a percentage of the property's equity towards a buyer's closing costs. Most lenders allow up to a 4% seller's concession. An example would be a buyer agreeing to pay a seller $100,000.

With the seller's concession, the purchase price would be $104,000 with $100,000 going to the seller and $4,000 going toward the closing costs. For this kind of transaction to work, the property would have to appraise for $104,000 or more.

Seller's concessions are popular in a buyer's market. A buyer's market is when there are more people selling their homes than people in the market to buy. It's called a buyer's market because sellers are competing for buyers' attention by offering more favorable terms and prices to beat out other sellers. A seller's concession can make a seller's property more attractive because they are allowing money that could have been profited to go towards a buyer's closing costs.

During a seller's market when there are more buyers looking for houses than houses being sold, sellers can demand the highest and best offer. If a buyer were to make an offer to a seller with a seller's concession, they could easily be beaten by someone who is offering to close using their own money.

A seller's concession can be a great option when available and during the right market. If you are in a hot market, a seller will more than likely put your offer on the bottom of the pile because they would prefer to cash out on every last dollar they can. On the other hand, when there are more houses than buyers, use the seller's concession to your advantage and finance the closing costs in your loan if the seller agrees.

Blueprint 4

Down Payment Assistance Works, If...
Sheek

A part of my life mission is to empower black homeownership around the country. My goal is to help increase black homeownership from 45% to 50% before I leave the planet. To achieve this, I have written this book, created an online course, developed a coaching program, and volunteered at home buying workshops. The Central Florida Urban League does a monthly home buyer class in which participants get a Down Payment Assistance Certificate.

The class has great teachers from different areas of the home buying journey. Unfortunately, many of the participants just are not ready to buy. Mostly because they do not really believe they can do it. They have obstacles or hear "no" and they retreat back into a tenant's reality instead of pushing forward into the home buyer's possibilities. Month after month we would have a room full of 50 people who invest eight hours of their Saturday to complete this course. The success rate of the attendees who actually purchased a home was abysmal.

That's what made Sheek stand out. When I walked into the class, it was like Sheek was vibrating at a different level than everyone else in the room. She felt confident, assured, and super optimistic. There was something different about her and I had to find out why.

When my section about credit and mortgage financing was done, I walked over to her and said, "You're really going to buy a house, aren't you?" She said, "Yes I am! I'm in contract right now but I need to take the class again because my down payment certificate is about to expire." It made sense. She saw this as the next step in her process. She wasn't looking for direction, validation, or motivation. Sheek was ready and this was one more thing she had to check off the list.

There are so many moving parts in this process. It can be intimidating. What worked for Sheek is she had a clear purpose and vision for homeownership. "I had no clue what to do to buy a house. All I knew was my girls were getting older and I wanted something different for them than what I had. I did not want them to feel like they did not belong anywhere or feel like they were not worthy of whatever they wanted in their lives. How could I tell them they could do whatever they wanted, when I could not see it in myself? When I made up my mind, that was it. I worked on everything I needed to do. None of it came easy, but it wasn't hard because I already made up my mind. I just had to do what I had to do."

Those words really resonated with me. Far too many people who go to those classes use the class to say, "I can't do that." With Sheek, it was "I'm going to do this."

I asked her, "What is the secret to how you are able to get past all your obstacles to get to your goal?"

She replied, "If all these people out here can do it, I had to be able to figure it out. It did not matter if it was a few months or a few years. I just decided to do it. Now I cannot believe I'm so close to closing."

"What do you think this will mean for your daughters?"

Through an emotional smile Sheek said, "It's a new life. They were there with me through the bad times and now they get to walk through the doors of the house with me. I want them to know they can do anything they believe they can do. I want them to be proud of their mother. I'm proud of myself and I can't wait to close and to move in."

Blueprint for Down Payment Assistance

1. Go to HUD.gov to find Down Payment Assistance programs in your state.
2. Make sure you meet the credit, income, and household size requirements for your down payment needs.
3. Find a HUD Housing Counseling agency to work with.
4. Complete the 8-hour home buying class certified by a HUD Housing Counseling agency.
5. Submit offers on multiple properties at a time. Offers including a down payment certificate are less likely to be accepted than others. Patience and persistence are required.

CHAPTER 5

Unlocking the Right Home

Finding "home" can be a comforting experience, yet the process comes with its twists and turns. At some points home buyers can feel a range of emotions from excited to exhausted. You may think that you found the perfect home only to find out that someone outbid you at the last minute, or the property needed more work than expected. These are the kinds of disappointment one can feel during their search.

Other times it will feel like absolutely everything is falling into place and finally you open the door to your new home. Home buyers get to that ultimate goal through patience, perseverance, and purpose. How you choose to exercise those qualities can be applied to any means of finding the right place.

While many of the homes sold a year are done with the help of a real estate agent, on average 8% of residential real estate sales are For Sale By Owners (FSBOs). FSBOs, as they are called, are listed by the owner of the house. Some of these sellers are motivated by how quickly a buyer can close, and others are motivated by earning top dollar. Looking at the different ways you can buy property can give you ideas on how you may want to conduct the search for your home.

I was invited to do a credit workshop for a church. When I got to the church, instead of millennials and young married couples in the church there was a room full of church elders. I thought to myself, "What do they need credit help for?" Still, I took to the stage and gave the audience the best presentation I could do.

At the end, during a question-and-answer session, I began to get questions about ways the elders could help their children and grandchildren. Many of them were dismayed because the people who should have been there weren't focused and serious about building better credit or learning the steps to buying a house. Instead, elders who already owned what they owned and had no interest in buying anything new were the ones in attendance.

One lady raised her hand slowly and began to tell me how her friend passed away and her grandson didn't have credit and had little income, but he wanted to buy the house. I connected with him, yet soon realized he was in no position to stop the house from going up for a foreclosure auction. We made a deal, and I was able to buy the house from him and help him get a fresh start in a new home before this house was taken from him.

I did not go to that church as a home buyer or an investor but speaking to people the subject came up. Even if you are not ready just yet, start talking about your goals. If a neighbor is going through financial struggles and needs to sell their home, they're not going to shout it out from the front porch, but if they know you are looking to buy, you could be the one they choose to sell it to.

I have bought properties from real estate agents, from people at church, my barber, the hair salon (from when I had dreadlocks if you were wondering), from foreclosure lists, and referrals ranging from accountants to divorce attorneys. Your home could be anywhere and the more people you speak to about what you want, the more chances you have of getting what you want.

With your home search getting underway, it would be a huge benefit for you to be open to different ways and options to include in your quest.

Who is Selling Your Home?

Real Estate Agents

Real estate agents have access to the Multiple Listing Services. In any neighborhood in the country, an agent can input the details of the home you want to buy and generate a list that has the pool you want, the number of bedrooms and bathrooms, and the price range you can afford.

Working with a real estate agent can be a balancing act in which you tell them everything you want followed by an unrealistic expectation of how much you should pay for your dream. Then the agent gets to balance your emotions with reality and hope you're still there when they let you know how much what you want would cost.

First time home buyers should understand this may be the first home and it does not have to be the last. Most people in the homes you dream to live in began in a starter home, built equity, and then rolled it over into a bigger home. Approaching home buying in this manner allows buyers to do the most important thing. Get into a home. From there they will receive a crash course in Murphy's Law and learn how to deal with plumbing issues, air conditioning and heating issues, and everything else inside and outside of the home.

This is par for the course. A real estate agent will help you to temper your expectations and put the market you are searching in into perspective for you. An agent at times will be your friend, your guide, a thorn in your side, and your life coach when you face disappointment in your journey. They can be an invaluable resource who will take a lot of the pressures of this process off your shoulders.

For Sale By Owners (FSBO)

The other 8% of the home market is sold as For Sale By Owners. These are any transactions where the buyer and the seller work directly with each other to make the sale happen. In most cases these are the best deals to be found. This is because there is no realty fee or Realtor expertise to drive up the price. Also, many of these sellers have different motivations than conventional home sellers.

Why Would Someone Sell a House By Themself?

Each seller has a different motivation for selling their property. People who are planning to sell to upgrade or downsize generally can work with someone to make those goals come through. Other sellers include people who have inherited property, are facing foreclosure, or simply do not want to pay a commission to a professional.

For the latter group the speed of the sale may matter more than the price. One day while I was driving with my cousin Khalid, his phone rang. The voice on the car speaker sounded very eager and excited. Then my cousin heard the person say, "I will take your offer!" When he hung up the phone, I said, "Congratulations!" Khalid is a real estate investor and was about to have another flip under his belt.

The seller had been fighting to keep her investment property. The property was badly in need of repairs and after another bad tenant, they were ready to give it up. They tried to sell with a realtor, but the buyers couldn't get a mortgage on the property because it needed too much investment in repairs. They were now getting offers from investors. Currently there was another investor offering $10,000 more than Khalid. So, I asked him, "Why did she take your offer and leave $10,000 on the table?"

He said, "The other person she was working with needed too much time to close. I told her I could close in 10 days."

Speed is a huge factor with For Sale By Owners. The more distressed the scenario, the more speed matters. These are generally the best deals to be found on the market. It takes a financially strong investor to perform in such little time.

Types of FSBOs

Pre-Foreclosure

When a mortgage is in default, the lender will file a Notice of Default in the county clerk's office where the property is located. This is the legal process that will lead to a property being repossessed or foreclosed on. If the owner acts, they can save the property. This phase is generally known as a pre-foreclosure. This is the most in demand property type for real estate investors, and people who want to find a deal in real estate.

They are heavily sought after because a homeowner who knows they are in a race against time to find a solution for a property or lose it could be willing to take lower offers than other homeowners. As the process gets further along, a homeowner becomes more and more open to offers that are less than the property value.

Short Sales

A short sale is the sale of a property in which the owner owes more on the property than it is worth. This is also known as a house being "underwater." With this process, the lender works with the seller and reduces the amount of money they will accept to pay off the mortgage. They are willing to be a part of the solution because when they must repossess or foreclosure on a home, it hurts their financial projections. To avoid taking back the home, they take the loss on the amount owed and make it possible for more buyers to meet the short-sale price.

Foreclosure

A foreclosure is when a lender repossesses a property they made a loan on. For a buyer to buy a foreclosure, they would have to purchase it at a foreclosure auction or after the auction as a REO (Real Estate Owned by the bank). Once the bank owns a property, they are usually willing to sell it quickly at a discounted price. For a traditional buyer, it is difficult to buy a property at an auction because they would be competing with seasoned investors who are capable of closing with a cash offer in days rather than the weeks most buyers need.

In 2008 I lost a house to foreclosure. My tenants weren't paying and even though they were getting the notifications from the bank, they didn't tell me there was an auction date until it was too late. I knew I was well behind on the mortgage, but my head was in the sand because I just couldn't believe this was happening to me.

I tried to make a last-ditch effort to get it back at the foreclosure auction, yet as soon as the bidding started, it was out of my hands and when the gavel fell on the judge's desk, the devastation of losing a property set in. It was a surreal experience. The buyer paid cash the same day.

Probate

A probate occurs when someone passes away without a will and trust. The assets in the estate are allocated to the next of kin based on several factors. If there is real estate, it can be given to a relative or friend who lives near or far. For people who inherit properties that are in different towns or states, they can be highly motivated to sell as quickly as possible. Think about it. They are now responsible for a whole property and even get a tax bill. If they can't be near the property to make sure it is being looked after it can become a burden.

That's why probate real estate is where some of the deepest discounts in real estate are found.

Vacant

A vacant house is the number one sign of a potential deal. What can a seller of a vacant property say to convince you it is worth more? The challenge with vacant property is finding the owner since they obviously don't live at the property. Also, many vacant properties have gone through the foreclosure process and are owned by the bank. When they are owned by the bank, the general public usually won't get a chance to make an offer on the property.

There are a multitude of avenues to take to get to your home. Gain clarity on how much time you must invest in the home search. The more time, money, and systems you have, the better the deal to be had. The best way to look at this is a real estate agent will allow you access to more houses to choose from but there will also be more competition for each house. More competition and more visibility usually equal a higher price. Finding a property by yourself will offer you less properties to look at and less competition. When a buyer can find an off-market property, the price is usually lower than those listed on the MLS.

Online Property Searches

Technology has changed the way real estate is conducted. Just a few years ago, it would be inconceivable to think someone could conduct a home search in another state without leaving the living room. With the resources available today, you can find out what properties are for sale in the area you desire. Real estate agents can give virtual home tours to clients they've never seen in person.

The benefit you have today is that home buyers have the tools at their fingertips to educate, inform, and empower them throughout the process.

When Sharon hit her 61st birthday she celebrated by starting her home search. She had lived in Brooklyn, New York since the 1970s and was ready to take her foot off the gas pedal in life and settle into a slower pace of living. Sharon was so ready to make the move to sunny Florida to have her dream home built, yet she had no clue where to start. We got her pre-approved for a mortgage, and I referred her to a Realtor who was an expert in new constructions.

The Realtor would FaceTime her and virtually take her to open houses. They did virtual tours in which Sharon would get a video recording of the property. She would get so excited and show her friends and co-workers the videos. She had a professional who cultivated a relationship with her and took the time to create a home buying experience that met her needs.

While other buyers were pulling out their hair in frustration, Sharon would wait in anticipation for the next virtual tour. She didn't have to sit in traffic, she didn't have to sacrifice her weekends, and she didn't have to drive around. All the properties came to her, so she was able to search for the perfect home with no pressure and tons of joy.

This is all possible because of the impact of technology on real estate. If a buyer doesn't know something, there is access to a professional with the click of a mouse. They can also utilize the many websites that are able to provide information from property value to taxes, and everything in between. Understanding how to navigate these sites puts a potential buyer in the driver's seat because they can speak to their real estate professionals from an informed and empower-ed stance.

Online Property Search Tools

Zillow

Zillow is the most popular online real estate information site available. They have an average of 1.8 million daily users. Zillow seems like such a staple in modern real estate culture. It was just

Unlocking the Right Home

PROPERTY VALUE SITES

Zillow – Zillow is the biggest player in the online house values game, through a feature called a "Zestimate," which is an automated estimate based on public records and sales comps. You can also search for "sold" listings to determine your own comps.

Trulia – Like Zillow, Trulia allows you to search "sold listings" to gather comps.

Redfin – An online brokerage with online property valuation tool.

Realtor – Realtor.com is now allowing you to search for your home's worth by showing what houses sold for in your area.

Property Shark – Property Shark provides public data on a property, recent sales, sale history, and comparables. No need to provide your contact info, either.
*Get paid subscription for best results

You can also use any online resource for the county that the property is in. New York City has ACRIS and Long Island, New York has www.mynassauproperty.com as great resources to research properties to find out comparable sales to help determine the value.

Pay Property Value Sites

Home Smart Reports
Home Smart Reports offers a pay house value engine including property information, nearby sales with map, and a neighborhood summary, as well as a much more advanced report with risk analysis, many more comps, and other statistical charts.

RealQuest
The RealQuest service (rated tops by several BP members) provides tons of useful data on a given property. Basics include Property Detail Report, Comparable Sales, Parcel Map/Assessor Map, Street Map, Neighborhood Information, Legal and Vesting, Automated Valuation (AVM), Transaction History, Custom Searches, and Flood Maps.

115

founded in 2006. This site allows people to "browse, buy, rent, sell, and more." Unlike the MLS which is exclusively accessed by real estate agents and brokers, Zillow is accessible to all. On the website you can search for properties based on address, zip code, and more.

One of the most important features Zillow offers is the information on property sales, and properties for sale. For a home buyer, knowing how much comparable sales are will guide how much you can expect to pay in a neighborhood. You can also get information about a property's square footage, year built, school district details, and other features.

A "Zestimate" is Zillow's estimate of how much a house is worth. While it is a good gauge of comparable prices, it is not as accurate as an appraisal. There are options to filter home searches by price ranges, property type, bedrooms, and bathrooms. This way you can see the different options as you add or remove features from the home search.

While Zillow is the most popular online home marketplace, there are others that offer a similar experience.

- Trulia
- Realtor.com
- Homesnap

- The Bottomline
- Neighborhood Scout
- Property Shark
- Geo Data

Understanding Home Values

A property appraisal is a report created by a licensed or certified property appraiser. The report gives their opinion of the value of the property (property value.) They base it on research done on the property including pictures, and an assessment of the condition of the home. The strongest factors that determine appraised value are comparable sales which are sales of properties up to a mile away from the property. They must share similar characteristics. Square footage, neighborhood, and age of the property are a few of the qualities appraisers consider in selecting a property to base the valuation on.

During the home buying process, the appraisal can make or break the deal. Most residential contracts of sale come with an appraisal contingency. It states that if the appraisal does not cover the price of the property, the buyer can get out of the contract without penalty. In a more aggressive seller's market, buyers may be forced to pay over the appraisal value as sellers may remove or reduce the impact of such contingencies.

Lenders rely on appraisal reports to determine how much they would be willing to make a loan for. Since they lend based on a percentage of the appraised value this process establishes the lending limits for the loan amount.

Making an Offer

Real estate is a numbers game. The more properties you see, the more offers you make. The more offers you make, the more likely you are to have offers accepted. There are times when buyers get their first offer accepted, but usually buyers must make offers on multiple properties to get one offer accepted.

The most successful offers are the ones that meet a seller's needs. As mentioned earlier, some sellers prioritize the highest price. Others may need to close quickly or need a buyer who will allow them time after closing to stay in the property. The more information you have about your seller, the better suited you will be to make an offer that hits home.

When making your next offer, follow this process to get your offer accepted.

Steps for Making an Offer on a House

1. Determine you can afford the house and decide to make an offer.

MAKING AN OFFER CHECKLIST

	Get Pre-approved by a lender.
	Ensure the property value justifies the purchase price. Have your Realtor do a Comparative Market Analysis and research the property value online.
	Make sure your down payment is in the bank and accessible. The money should include: initial deposit, down payment, and closing costs.
	Have necessary funds on hand to cover closing costs (usually between 3-5% of the purchase price).
	Have your good-faith deposit (earnest money) ready.
	Make sure your offer agreement details the terms of the earnest money, including its disposition upon the acceptance or rejection of the offer.
	Negotiate for the lender or seller to pay some of the closing costs. Ask your lender for a lender's credit in a seller's market. Request a seller's concession in a buyer's market.
	What contingencies will you include in your offer? They may include: · Final loan approval. · The home passing an inspection. · Repair, replacement, and/or improvement of issues revealed during the inspection. · Property appraisal to verify the home's value (required by lenders). · Is the purchase contingent upon the sale of a home you currently own? · Any other contingencies that your lender or state and local laws may require.
	Set up a clear time frame for the owner to provide disclosures regarding improvements and condition of the property. This could include natural hazards, neighborhood issues, homeowner association obligations, and more. Local and state laws might require additional disclosures as well.
	Optional: Enclose a personal letter to the owner. (Some buyers do this to explain the offer's price rationale — or to make a personal appeal for an offer to be given additional consideration).
	Set an expiration time and date for your offer. In a seller's market, this could be only a few hours. In most cases it's a few days.
	Set a time frame for a loan closing date (usually 30 to 60 days).
	Specify the number of days after closing that you may begin occupying the property, allowing time for an owner-occupied property to be vacated.
	In some states, it's required for a lawyer to review or prepare the written offer. Even if it's not required, it's a good thing to consider.

2. Talk with your real estate agent about comparable homes before making an offer.
3. Your real estate agent compiles a written offer.
4. The written offer is sent to the seller's agent.
5. The seller replies and your offer is accepted, countered, or declined.
6. Learn how to compete with multiple buyers.
7. The closing process begins when your offer is accepted.
8. Remember to negotiate before finalizing if contingencies reveal flaws with the house or deal.
9. Once your offer is accepted, finalize the contract.

Negotiating for Your Home

During the offer process, there will be opportunities to try to get the most out of your deal. Depending on the market you are in, it will determine how aggressively you can negotiate. In a seller's market, the seller holds all the cards. To offer below market value will most likely leave you on the outside looking in. Rather than negotiating against the seller, your negotiations are against the buyers who will be competing with you for a property. If you are working with a real estate agent, they will handle the negotiations. Nonetheless, it's important to have your goals be the real estate agent's guiding light while working for you. When buying a

Buyer's Market

**Buyers have more
bargaining power**

Seller's Market

**Buyers have less
bargaining power**

FSBO, you must be prepared to handle the ebb and flow of real estate negotiations. Some of the items that can be included in negotiation are:

- A larger deposit than requested
- Shortened inspection period
- Fast closing time
- Flexibility on when sellers must move out
- Waive contingencies (except appraisal unless you are willing to pay above market price)

Negotiating in a Seller's Market

Use what you have working for you. In a seller's market, the offers being submitted must be competitive on price. Where you can win could be with:

- A larger deposit than requested
- Shortened inspection period
- Fast closing time
- Flexibility on when sellers must move out
- Waive contingencies (except appraisal unless you are willing to pay above market price)

Rob and his wife Patricia found the perfect house. They had been looking at properties and making offers for eight months. Patricia was so exhausted from the process she was ready to take a break until the next year. Until now. Here was a property with the perfect size bedrooms, the perfect kitchen, and the backyard that reminded her of her childhood. Finally, she found all her needs and most of her wants in one property with a price that was more than reasonable.

She and Robert didn't want to wait, or risk losing this deal by haggling for a second. They jumped right in and offered $5,000 above asking price and waived the appraisal contingency. They had saved enough for the down payment plus some. The way they saw it, they were willing to pay more than the bank would lend them and it was worth it.

Rob looked at me and said, "How much would you pay to make your wife happy?"

I said, "I understand."

Every real estate transaction you make is at least part business. I recommend making sure the numbers work. For Robert and Patricia, it had become about more than money. It was about peace of mind. If they had to pay $5,000 for it, then this deal was a steal. I love a good negotiation. The worst thing you can do is to negotiate yourself out of the right deal. When real estate is at a premium because there is not a lot of housing inventory on the market, to find the house that fits your family may cost you more than you would hope to pay, but you must ask yourself one question.

"Would it hurt more to pay more, or to lose the right property?"

Timing is everything. As much as it may feel great to talk a seller down on their price, you must know when to hold them and when to fold them. In a seller's market when there are more buyers than sellers, be prepared to yield to make a deal.

The characteristics of a seller's market are:

- Demand is higher
- Inventory is lower
- Shorter listing times
- Multiple offers
- Higher offers

Negotiating in a Buyer's Market

In a buyer's market, sellers are more motivated to do what it takes to have you take their property off their hands. In this case, they are effectively negotiating against other sellers for your attention. The last strong buyer's market occurred after the Great Recession of 2008. After prices dropped drastically, sellers wanted to be able to get out before they lost more equity; however, there were only a few people prepared to buy. Banks were not lending money and only gradually extend programs for home loans. For a buyer, they had the chance to be aggressive with their offers. Instead of hoping their offer was high enough to compete, buyers were hoping their offers were not too low and that they offended the sellers.

When negotiating in a buyer's market, to win you can:

- Make low offers on multiple properties
- Include contingencies and clauses
- Get a seller's concession
- Offer a lower deposit

Jermaine was the first player back in the game. Many people got hit badly during the mortgage crisis. Some of my friends, partners, and associates lost houses and most everyone I knew in the real estate investment area lost income. Somehow Jermaine managed to pick himself up by wholesaling for cash buyers. He eventually was buying again himself.

He found a property in Long Island, New York whose owner was feeling the crunch. They were desperate to sell, yet they owed more than Jermaine was willing to pay. The owner decided they would give Jermaine the property for what they owed and not a dollar more. They were even willing to leave the furniture to sweeten the pot.

From the outside looking in, it may look like it was a bad deal by the seller, but every month that passed by was taking them deeper and deeper into a hole. Having the burden of the mortgage lifted was a huge relief. Even though they didn't walk away with any money, they were finally able to press the reset button and no longer had to fear losing the house to the bank. This is not uncommon in a buyer's market.

The characteristics of a buyer's market are:

- Demand is lower
- Inventory is higher
- Longer listing times
- Fewer offers
- Lower offers
- Price Reductions

Be prepared to buy. When you can buy when everyone else wants to sell, you're like the only person selling umbrellas in the storm. The most money is made in real estate when there is "blood in the water." What goes up must come down. If you are in a market that is up and you don't have to buy now, there is a good chance that if you wait, the market will shift, and better deals will show up. Only if there was a magic ball to let people know when the shift would happen.

In 2021, there was a nationwide seller's market. While some experts are projecting a turn in the market, the fundamentals of this market are very strong and don't show signs of slowing down. With the Covid-19 relief funds circulating, the moratorium on foreclosures and evictions, and a housing market built on more conservative lending practices than in the past, this market could stay strong with limited inventory for two years or more. Things could change with legislation to increase the rate of bank foreclosures or some unforeseen issues. Stay ready, so you won't have to get ready.

The Contract

A purchase and sale agreement or "The Contract" is more than a few sheets of paper. It is an instrument with significant power. It will include every detail of the purchase of your home. It is a binding agreement enforceable by law. Each state has its own contract template which includes the nuances in their law.

A standard contract will contain the typical purchase specifics, but the contract can include everything from the down payment to furniture to be included in the sale. The party in the position of power gets to dictate the terms of the contract. If the seller's property is in demand, they can request a higher down payment and a shorter inspection period.

When the buyer is in control, they can include escape clauses that allow them to get out of the deal for any reason they state in the contract. They can also request a seller's concession which when a seller is in demand would not typically happen. They would take the amount of the seller's concession (such as the seller paying the closing costs) as profit. When the seller must be flexible to make the deal work, the buyer can push the envelope on their demands. The contract is where this is done.

Some states require an attorney to be involved with a real estate closing because it can be more detailed than the average buyer may be prepared for. Whether your state requires an attorney or not, it is wise to seek legal counsel while purchasing a property. On one hand you want to make sure you are not signing something you don't understand. On the other hand, you want to make sure you get the most out of the transaction you can. A good attorney can help you do that.

Blueprint 5

Making "The" Decision
Kamilah

Kamilah is the newest homeowner of all the others highlighted. What her journey shows again, is the power of making the decision. The decision to become a homeowner is the first and biggest step in this entire process. Once you make the decision, you could be like Kamilah.

"When did you decide you wanted to become a homeowner?"

"I was renting a three-bedroom apartment in Queens, New York. I was expecting my daughter in 2017. When she came, we had just enough room. I realized time was running out and so was the space, because she and my son would not be able to share a room forever.

"At the time my credit was not the best and I did not have enough money for a down payment. I spoke to a friend, and she said, 'If you save up your next two tax refunds you will have the money for a down payment right there.' Before that conversation I thought I needed 20% and $100,000 in the bank and I did not have it. I thought, 'They're married, or their situation is different than mine. I'm not there yet. Suddenly I got curious about what it could be like to become a homeowner.'

"What's crazy is once I told a few people I wanted to buy a house; things just started to happen to make it work for me. One day my friend told me they were hiring at her job. She said, all I have to do is apply and I'll get it. I got the job and it helped me to save faster and make more money. That made me feel more comfortable about affording a house.

"Then the pandemic hit and as a nurse, I had nothing to do but work. I could not go anywhere to spend money, so it helped me to save even more. It also gave me the chance to watch your Facebook Lives, which felt like they were talking to me every time.

"Some of the other nurses at my job bought houses and they told me I could do it too.

"I started looking to rent a house in Rosedale, Queens, and when I told my co-workers what I was getting ready to pay, one of them said, 'Come to New Jersey and see what I own for as much as your rent would be.' For the same price of a small apartment, my coworker had a beautiful four-bedroom, two-bathroom house with an attached garage. The property was about 6,500 square feet so the backyard was huge. On top of that, everything was brand new. "When I saw what I could get on Zillow, I started window shopping and saving properties to look at.

"I started working on paying my credit card down and improving my credit. Now I was on the path, and I really felt like I could do it. But then I saw the prices going up. I started feeling anxious. I was thinking, if I don't get on this now, I'm not going to be able to buy at all. I added a few neighborhoods to my 'favorites,' so I watched the prices go up and started to work even harder to get ready.

"My friends at work started to ask me, 'When are you going to start looking?' I did not know what the next steps were, so my coworker gave me the number to her Realtor. They told me I had to get pre-approved, so I went online to find a lender.

"I connected with a lender who from the very beginning was condescending and difficult. She told me I should work with her Realtor and was pushy about it. I was worried I wouldn't be able to close without doing what she told me to do. Every house the Realtor showed me was terrible, but the lender and Realtor were pushing me to buy the Realtor's listings in places I didn't want to be in, rather than even showing me what I was asking for.

"I finally got fed up and fired the Realtor, but since I came so far, I was still working with the lender whose attitude was even worse now.

"I found a house I loved. I knew a lot of people wanted it, so I bid $65,000 over the asking price and someone still outbid me! I felt mad about that, but I kept on going. The new Realtor was showing me the types of houses I wanted in the areas I wanted to live in. My lender on the other hand kept telling me I shouldn't be looking for the houses I wanted because I 'had an FHA loan' and how sellers were not going to wait for me to close. Well, shortly afterwards I found someone who wanted to sell to me.

"The house was perfect. It had absolutely everything I was looking for. When I told my lender, she told me the rate was going to be 4.25% and it would cost me $1,800. She said her bank would not give me a loan without paying discount points. I didn't know any of my friends or coworkers who paid a 4% interest rate. It just didn't sound right to me. I ended up finding a lender who offered me a rate almost 2% lower. When I told my original lender about what I was being offered, she told me I shouldn't take the loan and her rate wasn't so bad. When I told her I was not going to work with her, she sent an email to the listing agent and all parties involved to paint me as a difficult borrower.

132

"I remember you said, 'Nobody can eat until I sign on the dotted line' during one of your Facebook Lives. When I heard that I felt empowered to call the shots on my loan and it was a big help. I went with the better deal and ended up saving over $400 a month because I didn't take the first thing offered to me.

"We closed on the house, and now I get to pull into my own garage. I get to see the children running around the backyard. We have rabbits and deer back there which is cool. It was really a journey, but we made it."

"What message would you give to people who are going through the home buying process?

If you're waiting for things to be perfect it will never happen. Just do it. Just try. There will always be bills, there will always be competition for a house. All that can happen is you get a yes or a no. We got no's, but I kept going until I got the yes I was looking for. You can too.

Blueprint for Home Loan Financing

1. Apply for a mortgage with a lender six months to a year before you plan on buying.
2. Request detailed suggestions to make you home loan ready.
3. Go through all your possible sources for a down payment (bank accounts, 401(k)s, IRAs, life insurance, DPA, etc.).
4. Determine your home loan payment limit and search for your home based on those numbers.
5. Make sure your real estate team is responsive and complying with deadlines.

THE MORTGAGE PROCESS

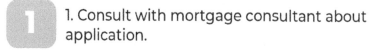

1. Consult with mortgage consultant about application.

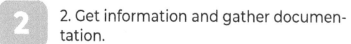

2. Get information and gather documentation.

3. Obtain pre-approval for loan.

4. Now find a home.

5. Have property inspection.

6. Lender will order third party services.

7. Buyer gets homeowner's insurance.

8. Get lender update.

9. Now it is time for the pre-closing review.

10. Now it is time for the escrow signing!

It is now time for the closing!

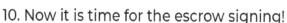

CHAPTER 6

Unlocking the Closing Process

Your Offer is Accepted...

Congratulations, and let's get to work! Once your offer is accepted by the seller, the clock is ticking for you to execute on this deal. Your contract with the seller will specify all the details of the sale to be met by the buyer and the seller. The contract will protect both parties and guide the way the deal will be conducted.

The key elements of the contract are:

- The purchase price
- Close by date
- Escrow deposit
- Inspection period
- Conditions for an extension
- Move out dates

A contract can get very detailed based on how savvy the buyer, seller, or representatives are. Ultimately, with these major items addressed, both parties are on track to get a deal done. As the buyer, once the seller signs the contract and accepts your deposit, you have rights by contract to close on the house. Even if another party came in with an offer significantly higher than yours, the seller would be obligated to work with you up until the date specified on the contract.

At this point you've done all the preliminary work. Now every step counts that much more. This is where dreams come true or are broken. Thanks to the help of a diligent real estate agent, if you use one, you are ready to take the next big step and get your other team members involved.

Your Mortgage Approval

To get "pre-approved," your lender would have required a full application, a credit report, and supporting income documentation to get you started. With all your documentation on hand, a lender would need to get a copy of your contract and updated paperwork to officially submit a loan to their underwriting department for a "Conditional Loan Approval."

The next step is to go from being "pre"-approved to being "approved."

Conditional Loan Approval

There is a wide variety of mortgage programs available for home buyers. They cater to the different needs buyers have. For traditional buyers, programs like FHA and Conventional Mortgages offer homebuyers the luxury of only having to put down a minimum of 3.5-5% as a down payment on their home. Other buyers, such as business owners, may have to qualify for a loan that requires a larger down payment, and more documentation, to prove their income.

Once the required documentation, credit, and contract are submitted to an underwriter, there are options to follow. The first option is the loan is denied. This can happen if the buyer does not meet the standard set for debt-to-income ratios, reserves in their account, or credit to name a few. Any factor in the home buying journey can cause a loan to be denied, but to get a loan approved, all those factors must meet the guidelines.

When a buyer's income, credit, and money meet the lending guidelines, they are issued a "Conditional Loan Approval!" At this point, you are on your way to the closing table if you can verify the details from your application. Lenders are very meticulous in their review of files. Even though they would have received tax returns, and pay stubs to prove a buyer's income, they are still going to do a Verification of Employment by contacting your employer.

Even though they received your bank statements, they're going to request the latest one to make sure the money which was there before is still there before closing. To get a Conditional Loan Approval, the lender would have signed off on what is on the credit report, but they're going to ask you to explain past delinquencies or issues to make sure you are indeed credit worthy.

While this process has been called "annoying, or frustrating," you are weeks or days away from this process financing your dream. Stay focused and cooperate with your lender to get everything done as quickly as possible. Make yourself available by phone, text, email, and smoke signal if you need to. Things will be moving quickly at this point so move urgently to address anything your loan officer requests. They are not doing it for the fun of watching you chase paper. They are crossing "T's" and dotting "I's" so you can get your keys.

About two years after the Great Recession, banks were back to lending, but man was it difficult. They were like someone who got heartbroken and had trust issues. They questioned every single late payment that appeared on a credit report. They scrutinized every document for an unreasonable period of time. They rejected appraisals left, right, and center, so actually getting a loan to close was quite the feat.

I got a call from a potential client. Let's call her "Sonya." Sonya was so excited because while other people's businesses and finances were in the gutter, she had experienced the most prosperity in her business. She did IT for a big accounting firm. She now was the belle of the ball because every seller she met rolled out the red carpet to invite her in and offer her their home. There were so few qualified buyers who were ready to step back into the ruins of the real estate market. For each one who did, they had their pick of the best properties at the best price.

Sonya was thoroughly enjoying the process until she got into contract and needed the mortgage to close. She was approved for a loan with 10% down, which was not a problem for her. However, the underwriting process was a nightmare. The bank asked her to explain late payments that had been made over six years earlier. They questioned what seemed like every deposit and withdrawal from her bank statement. They found a problem with the appraisal and demanded the appraiser go back to the house to take more pictures and do more work which cost Sonya each time.

Sonya went from answering my phone calls with joy and anticipation, to answering with a "what do you want now" energy. She may have actually said it a few times too. She was getting burnt out by the constant requests, and explanations, followed by more requests to explain what she just explained. It was a ridiculous exercise. After a while, she just refused to cooperate. She told me, "This is the last time I'm sending anything to any of y'all."

She meant it. When I got the call that now the underwriter wanted this, that, and the next, I knew the loan was done. She never answered or returned my calls again. I do not know if she ever closed on the house or any others, but she definitely did not close with me.

Fortunately, banks are not nearly as difficult to deal with today. If your loan is becoming a burden, take a deep breath and remember why you are doing this. Think about all the lives that will be positively impacted by you taking this big step in your life. At this point you are so close, and nothing but a "no" from the bank should stop you from getting what you need to get to complete the process and get over the finish line.

Loan Estimate

A Loan Estimate takes you through the most important details about a mortgage loan you are applying for. It is the tool to help you understand what everything from the interest rate to the closing cost will be. This document is an estimate and must be sent to you within three days of your loan application being submitted. The purpose of it is to give you clear language and information whether you are purchasing a new home or refinancing a home.

If you notice something different on the Loan Estimate than what you have discussed with your lender, ask why. The best way to shop for a mortgage is to get Loan Estimates from more than one source. This way you will be able to compare loan offers to make the best decision.

The Loan Estimate is not an approval or denial of your loan. It is issued in the early phase of the loan process to give you information before you must invest in an appraisal or an inspection. It is designed to give consumers the information they need to make an educated decision outside of the words of a mortgage salesperson.

If there are significant changes made to your loan, a Revised Loan Estimate will be sent to you by hand or by mail. This prevents a consumer from being blindsided at closing. A loan company cannot change your interest rate, closing cost, or put you into a different loan program without giving you a revised estimate so you can see the changes.

Fixed vs. Adjustable Mortgage

One of the most vital features the Loan Estimate highlights is whether your loan is fixed or adjustable. A fixed rate mortgage has principal and interest payments which will remain the same for the life of the loan. Even though payments may increase or decrease over time because of the taxes, insurance, and mortgage insurance, the amount going to the bank will remain fixed. This is the best for buyers and homeowners who are not planning on selling or refinancing in the near future. These loans offer security and stability.

An adjustable-rate mortgage can change with the market. Most adjustable-rate mortgages are fixed for a period of time. For a savvy home buyer who plans to move or refinance within a few years, they can apply for a mortgage which is fixed for five years or ten years and subject to change thereafter.

The reason for this is adjustable-rate mortgages have lower interest rates than their more conservative counterparts. Only take an adjustable-rate mortgage if you are confident in plans to move or refinance in the near future.

30-Year vs. 15-Year Mortgage

Traditional mortgages come with one of two primary loan terms. A 30-year mortgage which offers a lower payment option or 15-year mortgage which offers a shorter loan term. A 15-year mortgage term is touted by many financial experts as the best loan option. It would have you own your home free and clear of any loan in half the time of a 30-year loan. It also comes with a lower interest rate. The difference between the interest paid on a 15-year versus a 30-year mortgage could be tens or hundreds of thousands of dollars depending on the size of the loan.

A 30-year mortgage is significantly more popular with consumers despite the extra interest. It offers a lower monthly payment since the payments are stretched over 30-years rather than 15-years. It allows buyers to have more purchasing power in the home buying market. For the 15-year mortgage buyers, their higher monthly payments qualifies them for a lower purchase price.

While there is a huge gulf in savings over time between the two, knowing whether saving money now or over time is most important will guide your decision to take out a 15-year or 30-year mortgage.

According to Juan Carlos Cruz, founder of Britewater Financial Group, "One option is to get a 30-year mortgage that doesn't have any prepayment penalties, then calculate what your payment would be if you had a 15-year mortgage and start by paying that amount monthly. This will reduce the principal faster and save a lot of interest, but it leaves you a way out if money unexpectedly tightens later on down the line. If you do this method, you can always revert to the smaller monthly payment if you face financial hardship," Cruz says. "You can move between the two payments without ever needing to refinance, which would also save you thousands in closing costs."

Bi-Weekly Payments

The strategy Juan Carlos Cruz details is one where the homeowner can control the path to being free and clear of a mortgage. A more conventional way of reducing the time left to pay on your mortgage is through bi-weekly payments. If a borrower pays half of a mortgage payment every two weeks, they would have paid an extra payment by the end of the year.

The purpose of doing this is to make an extra payment each year. You can technically do this however you choose. You can send a whole extra payment to the bank each year. You can divide the extra payment over 12 months and pay that way.

By doing this consistently, the mortgage would be paid off in about 24 years instead of 30 years. Using the example of a $2,000 a month payment, you would save about $144,000 by cutting out 6 years of interest on a mortgage. This is a powerful way to build wealth. The more paid to principle, the less interest can be charged. Sending one extra payment a year can have a significant impact. Think about what would be possible if you could send two extra payments a year!

Closing Disclosure

"Chad, your clients are here for the closing. Go up to the fourth floor and bring back the HUD!" said Ted like a rallying cry.

"Are you sure all of the numbers are the same as what I told them?" I asked with nervous excitement.

"Of course! Just don't come back if you don't close it," was Ted's reply.

This was my first closing, and I knew I was on the brink of something major. It was three months from me walking into that basement office with the energy, language, and smell of a "Boiler Room" where sales were made, and promises were broken.

Like Ted said, my clients were waiting for me on the fourth floor. That was the only thing he was honest about. When the lawyers pulled out the closing documents, the 6.5% I told them was 7%, and the fixed rate they demanded was fixed for only two years and adjustable afterwards! How could this happen?

I ran downstairs to fix it and was met by an evil grin. "Did you see the fee? Do you want it or not?" Ted asked with a confident "you know you want it" look on his face. I did! I did want it! I stood to make $3,000 on one deal! This would be more money than I'd ever held at one time.

I went upstairs and lied and lied and lied until they signed. They left disgruntled and I came back to the office with the HUD (HUD-1 settlement statement). I was so happy! I came back to a hero's welcome. Ed cut my tie and put it up on the wall with all the other closers. I was one of the boys, only there was the small detail of totally blindsiding an innocent couple into a loan they didn't sign up for. They had plans to save money and turned to me for help. Instead of helping them, I conned them into a subprime loan that was nothing like the Good Faith Estimate they received. But what could they do? Psychologically once someone comes to a closing with the intention of signing, they almost always will. This couple was no different.

I can honestly say I did not know that was going to happen. The first time. Afterwards, my conscience was numbed by chunks of money at a time. I learned how to do mortgages the wrong way and I taught others the same. The crazy thing is most of our clients came to us from other lenders who had lied to them.

The mortgage industry was the Wild West, and it went from 19-year-old newbies like me at the time, all the way up to the wealthiest institutions being complicit in bankrupting the country. The industry had to change. It was costing people their houses and others their integrity and reputation.

In 2015 mortgage loan disclosures underwent a sweeping change. The result was that people could no longer be given Good Faith Estimates that were different from the closing documents. They were now given a Loan Estimate. If there was a change in interest rates, closing cost, or any other material details of the loan, the Loan Estimate had to be disclosed to include those changes.

The Closing Disclosure took the place of the HUD-1 Settlement Statement. Borrowers in the past did not see the HUD-1 until the closing, which led many to be bamboozled at the last minute. The new law required all lenders to send borrowers the Closing Disclosure at least three days prior to closing. Now borrowers were able to review the documentation and have a trusted advisor review it without the pressure of having to close now or risk losing out.

The Closing Disclosure is the full breakdown of all a loan's material facts. This is a part of the Know Before You Owe initiative. Consumers are protected and the numbers are there for them to see.

The way of the old days did not go unpunished. Even though I managed to stay clear of any legal issues, many of my contemporaries sunk deeper into white collar crimes. Lying to people about the details of the biggest investment in their lives was a gateway for many to do worse. Personally, I learned from this and paid cosmically with bad karma as everything went wrong for me for years. I lost a house to foreclosure, faced financial ruin, and even got sick with a thyroid disease that brought my weight down to 129 pounds at one point.

God doesn't like ugly, and the mortgage industry was hideous.

With those hard lessons learned, I'm grateful to be able to take my lessons and bless others with information and insight which I've earned over time.

Title Company

How do you know the person selling a house actually owns the house? As a real estate investor, I've seen property pass from one person to another, with each person claiming to be the rightful owner. The way that debate is settled is through the title company. Title companies certify the ownership of a property based on public records.

They research all the details of a property from ownership to liens, to legal boundaries. While appraisers validate the value of a property, and an inspector validates the structural integrity of a property, the title company validates the history of a property. Before a bank will allow you to close on a property, they require a title report.

In the title report, the title company compiles how much is owed for taxes, when they are due, and how much money should be held at closing to establish an escrow account for your mortgage payments including taxes and insurance. They also show the chain of title which is a history of the past owners of the property including a record of how much each purchased and sold the property for, along with the dates they closed.

Buying a house without running a title report is like driving a car without brakes. It costs money upfront to get a title report, but what it saves you is invaluable. The title company has a fiduciary respon-sibility to convey a clean title to a new buyer. If there are disputes that arise over ownership or property lines, a title company would require this matter to be resolved before they issue title insurance and allow the deal to close.

Title insurance, like property insurance, is required on every bank closing to ensure there are no surprises popping up to challenge the bank's investment. This is a great way to learn more about the property you are purchasing. Consumers generally do not get a copy of the title report but the information inside can offer good insight on the property being bought.

Closing Costs

There are many moving parts going into you becoming a homeowner. Aside from the inspector and appraiser most of the fees charged are collected at closing. The Closing Disclosure is an itemized list of all the costs of the loan. They appear on page two of the Closing Disclosure and have 11 sections:

Unlocking the Closing Process

A. Origination Charges
B. Services Borrower Did Not Shop For
C. Services Borrower Did Shop For
D. Total Loan Costs (Borrower-Paid)
E. Taxes and Other Government Fees
F. Prepaids
G. Initial Escrow Payment at Closing
H. Other
I. Total Other Cost (Borrower-Paid)
J. Total Closing Costs (Borrower-Paid)
K. Subtotals (D + J)

Section A, Origination Charges, is where the lender charges their fees. They usually charge an application fee, underwriting fee, plus other miscellaneous charges. They can also charge points for the rate or a direct fee. Lender closing costs are an important area to compare mortgage companies on. The Loan Estimate will allow you to compare, so when the actual fees appear on the Closing Disclosure, you know you have closed on the best deal.

At this point you are a few pen strokes away from having your title change from renter to homeowner! If you have gone through this process and followed these steps, your life is changing and the possibility for self-determination and wealth have opened up to you.

Congratulations on getting to this point!

As vital as it is to follow the right path to get to your goals, a wise person learns from the mistakes of others. Here are some things NOT to do to make sure you don't take yourself off course.

Just DON'T DO IT!!!

We were about a week or so from clearing the file for closing. My client came to my office to get his original documents. I told him I would meet him in the front of the office building. I got there just in time for him to pull up in a brand-new white BMW. When he jumped out of the car, I said, "Nice whip! I didn't know you had this."

He said, "Yeah, I just got it!"

The look on my face went from vehicular admiration to a "oh no, you didn't." I couldn't believe he risked his chance of getting into a home to buy this car. I knew if the underwriter got a whiff of this, the deal would be dead. Think about it. With a new car payment comes a few hundred dollars on his DTI (debt-to-income) ratio. Also, when you run your credit for a car, you take on a new inquiry or a bunch of new inquiries.

That's exactly what happened with my client. When I finally got the call, my head sank, and I had to say goodbye to my closing. Worst still, my client had to go back to being a tenant until he improved his debt-to-income ratio. He was right at the finish line and took an unfortunate turn I wasn't at the time wise enough to warn him against.

10 Things NOT to Do When Buying a House

- Quit your job
- Get a new car lease or loan
- Take out new credit cards
- Buy furniture
- Co-sign for a credit card
- Miss a payment of any kind
- Spend your down payment money
- Make cash deposits over $1,000
- Close any credit cards
- Send out invitations to your housewarming before you close

Avoid these costly mistakes and you won't have to defer your home buying dreams. Unfortunately, people have killed their own dreams by making these mistakes. Learn from them so you don't have to put off home ownership. Your time is now!

Blueprint 6

Taking a New Path
Omari and Jodi

Omari is a brother to me. He and his wife Jodi decided to leave their families, friends, and me in New York to move to North Carolina. They were spending over $2,000 a month renting for a not so nice house in a not so nice neighborhood. They got sick of it and wanted a change.

When I spoke to Jodi about their experience she told me, "We were paying so much money and we couldn't even send our daughter to school in the school district. It made no sense."

I was like, "But Jodi, did you really have to leave your family, friends, and New York to find what you wanted?"

"For what we pay for a mortgage, we would have only been able to rent a tiny place in a rough neighborhood. Moving to Charlotte, North Carolina gave us options that New York couldn't in that price range." She continued, "Now we have a four-bedroom house, with everything brand new. We have a big backyard and a big house. We're in a growing city that does not offer as much as New

156

York in terms of dining options or nightlife, but for us and our two girls, we're in the perfect place."

"What was the biggest sacrifice you had to make to get to your home?" I asked Omari.

"My family. Leaving my mother, father, siblings, and friends was hard on me. I was the first one in my family to move away. Now we're looking to buy another house and rent out this one. Since I don't have that fear of leaving, we have the whole map as an option."

"What's your favorite part of being a homeowner?"

"Having the peace and privacy of your own home. In an apartment, sometimes you must tiptoe around. My daughter likes to sing at the top of her voice for no reason, and she can do that because this is her house. We're free to do what we want, have as much fun as we want."

I asked, "What's the best part of leaving where you're from?"

"We created another lane for the family. Our family gets to see a different part of the country and stay as long as they want. All they have to do is jump on a plane or take a drive and they have a new place at their fingertips. We get to go back as often as possible. Also, with the money we saved on buying a nice house for half the price of a similar one in New York, we get to travel all the time and have as much fun as we want. We go away at least once every three months. We only get to do that because we own our own home and we bought it right."

I then asked, "What does it mean for your children?"

"Jodi and I have a lot of equity in our house now and our girls are still young. We always wanted to be able to give them a start in life when they grew up. We've already done that. Now we get to see how much wealth we can earn with this house and others we plan to buy by the time they're grown. I don't know how else we would have been able to do it."

Homeownership opens so many doors. Sometimes to get to those options you may have to leave the comfort of what you knew as home. As you develop equity, you build wealth. Once you know what matters to you, you can use homeownership as a springboard to get there.

Blueprint for Buying in a New City

1. Determine what locations can give you the most of what you want in your next home.
2. Consider which regions of the country you and your family would like to live in.
3. Research the most important details for you in each city (average income, schools, taxes, crime, etc.).
4. Physically and/or virtually visit the top three contending cities to get a feel for your possible new home.
5. Be willing to leave the familiarity of a city or state if it cannot give you what you need as a home buyer.

CHAPTER 7

Unlocking Real Estate Investing

When you close on your first home, you enter a new level in your life. This success will have a ripple effect over generations of your family. The first house is the most important piece of a family's wealth because it can be the springboard to many more. The options for your next real estate steps are endless. With the topics to follow, you can explore the ideas you most resonate with.

I know we should let you move in, get settled down, and enjoy the housewarming for a bit. You deserve it. Still, we want you to start considering the new possibilities in your life because of this house. Home prices generally increase year after year. As you develop equity in your property, more and more chances to build wealth will appear.

Refinance

One of the best ways to access the equity in your home is to refinance. Refinancing is the process of taking out a loan on a property you own. A cash out refinance allows an owner to take out the equity they have built in their house based on the lender's guidelines. These funds can be used to purchase an additional property. Once you close on your first property, a cash-out refinance may not be an option for the first few years. As the property value increases, more and more equity will build up. When you have built up enough equity, you can review your options to make sure this is the best path for you.

Buying More Property

Getting a home loan for your second property is going to be significantly more challenging than the first one. The lender is taking more risk to do a loan for an investment property. As a result, they require stronger credit, more income, and a larger down payment. There are still many options to making it work and I want to highlight the most common challenges before giving some solutions. When you have a loan reporting on your credit there are a few things that will be going against you.

A mortgage is going to cause a huge jump in your gross monthly debt. Since DTI is a function of the gross monthly debt divided by the gross monthly income, the equation will be out of whack if another mortgage was added.

Example with One Mortgage

Gross Monthly Debt: $3,000
(Including first home mortgage)
Gross Monthly Income: $6,500

Debt-to-Income ratio ($3,000/$6,500=.46): 46%
This works!

REFI BENEFIT WORKSHEET

Balance Left on Loan	
Months Left on Current Loan	
Interest Rate on Current Loan	
Monthly Payment on Current Loan	
Total interest to be paid on remainder of Loan Term	
New Loan Amount	
Length of New Loan (months)	
New Mortgage Interest Rate	
New Mortgage Monthly Payment	
Total Interest to be Paid on New Mortgage	
Difference in Total Interest Payments	
Closing Costs for New Loan	
Points	
Appraisals	
Legal	
Inspections	
Credit Check	
Title	
Application fee	
Other	
Other	
Other	
Total Closing Costs for New Loan	
Monthly Payment Savings	
Time Period to Break Even From New Loan	

Example with Two Mortgages

Gross Monthly Debt
(Including first home mortgage): $3,000
+ Investment property mortgage: $1,500
= $4,500

Updated Gross Monthly Debt
(Including 1st and 2nd home mortgages): $4,500
Gross Monthly Income: $6,500

Debt-to-Income ratio ($4,500/$6,500=.69): 69%
This does NOT work!

To combat the DTI issue, an investment property buyer can use the projected rents from one property as income. This will lower the debt-to-income ratio and make it possible for the buyer to meet the DTI guidelines for a loan.

Buying a home for a primary residence is a world away from buying an investment property. While lenders make the barrier to entry reasonable for first-time buyers and people buying their primary home, an investment loan has much higher hoops to jump through. With proof of a primary mortgage on the credit report, a buyer will be asked to put down 20% or more to buy the second home.

If purchasing a property with someone else, you can use one person on the loan if they qualify by themselves. If this is possible, you can double your collective purchasing power as both parties will be on the title but only one would have the liability of the mortgage on their credit. This way, instead of the next property purchased having to qualify as an investment property with a 20% down payment or more, the person without a loan could qualify with a much lower down payment. Be mindful of owner occupancy requirements as this will determine if or how you can do this. Your lender could give you the specifics of how to make this work if it's possible for you.

BRRRR Method

Anyone can eventually buy a house. Not as many people buy an investment property. It would take a significant amount of time to save enough money for a down payment. When you can roll the equity from your first property into your second property, it may not take as long as you think. As the equity builds in your home, your property becomes a savings account. The BRRRR Method is an investment strategy that gives new homeowners a clear path to buying one house after another.

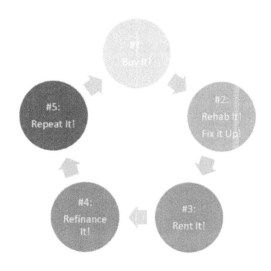

THE BRRRR METHOD

A great way to build wealth – Buy, Rehab, Rent, Refinance, Repeat!

Follow these steps:

- **Buy**: Purchase a distressed property with financing from a private or hard money lender.
- **Rehab**: Make improvements to the house to add value and get it ready to rent.
- **Rent**: Rent the property out at market rate.
- **Refinance**: Use a cash-out refinance to pay off your original private or hard money loan.
- **Repeat**: Use the profit from the cash-out refinance as a new down payment for your next investment property.

We threw on a bonus "R" in "Repeat" to show you are able to do this over and over again. You don't have to be rich, but you must move wise. The BRRRR Method offers homeowners a way to build cash flow and equity on as many properties as possible. All coming from cash-out refinance on one home and not just your bank account. This method puts the possibility for wealth in anyone's hands.

Rental Property

Rental property is the gift that keeps giving. Once you make the investment to buy and renovate a property, if necessary, your tenants will deposit money into your bank account month after month. Therefore, real estate offers a path to wealth other vehicles cannot. A good tenant is a gold mine for a landlord. The process of acquiring a property after you have purchased your first home is the key challenge to overcome. Throughout this chapter there will be options, resources, and strategies shared that will make this a formality with proper planning.

There are many ways to use rental property to exponentially increase your net worth. You can build wealth with single family homes, multi-family homes, and even rental arbitrage. Each of these avenues offer the opportunity to generate monthly cash flow, build equity, and get tax savings. With all the options avail-

Unlocking Real Estate Investing

RENTAL PROPERTY INCOME & EXPENSE WORKSHEET

Name: _____

1st Property Address: _____
    City: _____ State: _____ Zip: _____

2nd Property Address: _____
    City: _____ State: _____ Zip: _____

3rd Property Address: _____
    City: _____ State: _____ Zip: _____

Income	1st property	2nd property	3rd property
Rents Received			
Other Income			
Expenses			
Advertising			
Auto			
Cleaning and Maintenance			
Commissions			
Insurance			
Legal and Other Professional Fees			
Management Fees			
Mortgage Interest			
2nd Mortgage Interest			
Other Interest			
Repairs			
Supplies			
Utilities			
Phone			
Power			
Water			
Garbage			
Other Expenses			
Purchase Date of Rental Home or Date Property Became a Rental			
Purchase Price of Rental or Value When Property Became a Rental			
Value of Land or Lot Home is on			

By signing this worksheet you are agreeing that the information is correct to the best of your knowledge and contains no known false information designed to cheat the IRS.

Signature _____   Signature _____

169

able to you, gaining clarity on what would fit your lifestyle and life goals best is the place to start.

The Rental Property Income and Expense Worksheet shows some things to consider when deciding where to start.

Single Family Homes

The core benefit of purchasing a single-family home for rental income is the cost to buy it. Lenders will require 20% down for a loan on an investment property. When you consider the cost of a single-family home compared to a multi-family property, the down payment alone could represent a huge difference in the price of entry. With a lower price, you will also have a lower monthly payment.

Renting single family homes gives you the option to rent to college students on a room-by-room basis. You can rent to section 8 tenants whose rent is paid by the government. You could even rent the house out to seniors or disabled individuals which could require staff but higher potential profit margins. The ways you can make money on one property are vast. You can even "house hack" and rent out one unit or bedroom in your house while you live in another area of the house.

On the downside of building wealth through single-family homes, if you have one tenant and they leave, 100% of your rental payment leaves with them. Having one income from the property makes the landlord dependent on one tenant. If a tenant stops paying, not only does the money stop flowing to you, but it also starts flowing to attorneys for evictions, and to the bank because you are still responsible for the payments. This emphasizes the need to properly screen a tenant before you let them into the house. Because of this, single-family homes are good but limited in how well they can help you to become wealthy in real estate.

Multi-Family Property

Multi-family properties usually have one roof but many doors. Each door represents a stream of income. They allow investors to generate income by renting out each unit. The more units, the more income potential. This is an area in real estate that intimidates many. The belief is since they can be so lucrative and cost so much you can only buy multi-family properties if you are rich.

One of my mentors, Phil Georges, has been investing in multi-family real estate since 1986. He teaches a class called "How To Graduate to Multi-family." One thing he emphasizes is it takes as much work, and effort, to close one single-family property as it does for him to buy a 50-unit apartment building.

I asked Phil, "What are the main reasons people should consider multi-family investing?" He said, "Real estate is the cornerstone of wealth. Ninety percent of the wealthiest people in the world have significant amounts of real estate as part of their investment portfolio. Residential real estate is one of the most stable assets when it comes to investments. After all, people will always need a place to live. Should real estate investment become a passion, you will eventually acquire several more properties.

By the time you are comfortable and have 10 properties, you will hit a roadblock since lenders will cap lending around ten loans. Have no fear, at that time or sometime sooner is when you want to go into multi-family real estate for several reasons. For one there are no limitations on how many properties you can acquire. For me, it made more sense to have ten properties in one location as opposed to 10 different neighborhoods. Other reasons include vacancy percentages. In a single-family when you have a vacancy you are 100% vacant which means all the bills come out of your pocket. If you have one vacancy in your ten-unit property your vacancy rate would only be 10% and you still have ninety percent of the income to pay the bills."

With multi-family real estate, having a mentor like Phil can help you to leverage his experience so the details, the money, and the execution of larger deals are not so scary.

Rental Arbitrage

Vacation rentals are a booming market. In areas near the beach or any major attraction, homes are in demand to rent on a short-term basis. People are no longer confined to booking hotels. Many are interested in living in an area even if for a few days. Vacation rentals make that a reality. Guests from all over the world can request access to the home you have made available for them to rent during their vacation. The best part about this investment lane is you do not have to own the property.

Rental arbitrage is the process of renting a property, then subletting it to guests for a higher price than you pay. Vacation rental companies like Airbnb, and VRBO make it possible for the everyday homeowner or renter to provide an experience to travelers and make a significant profit doing it. This is a great strategy for an investment property. It also offers a unique opportunity which requires a deposit and rental payments opposed to a down payment and a loan. People with poor credit or limited funds can generate monthly cash flow on real estate by earning rental arbitrage, and you can too.

Flipping Houses

Do you remember Bob Ross? He was a painter who used to come on public broadcast television. He would take a blank canvas and paint a masterpiece every episode. It was so cool to watch this empty space turn into an amazing work of art. That's the same way I felt watching "Flip This House," which is a reality show about flipping real estate. The star of the show, Than Merrill, would find a house in bad condition. He would take a construction crew into the house. They would tear the house down to the studs and then you would see a beautiful home come to completion.

Flipping or "rehabbing" a house could be a lucrative project. Unlike rental properties where you make modest and consistent income monthly, house flipping offers a hefty payday if done right. If you feel like finding your first house has a lot of moving parts, add in everything you need to fix a house, plus everything you need to do to sell a house, and a cushion on each side in case of the challenges that will come up. Flipping is not for the faint of heart.

To successfully flip a house, you first must find a property at around 65% of the after-repair value of a comparable property in good conditions, minus the repairs required to have it meet market standards. If a rehabber buys a property for too much money, they risk losing a lot of money. It's important a rehabber has done their due diligence on the area sales so they know how much they need to buy the house for, how much money they can put into renovating it, and be clear on what they need to sell it for to make the profits they want.

A good house flip can yield a payday of tens of thousands of dollars or even six figures in one deal. It could also cost an investor hundreds of thousands of dollars if they get it wrong. The risk is high and the reward even higher. Like every area of real estate, the financing is what can make or break the deal.

Many house flippers use hard money loans which are high interest, short term loans to finance the purchase and in some cases, the repairs, on the property. Since many houses being rehabbed need major repair, they do not usually qualify for bank financing. Investors turn to hard money loans which are short term, high interest real estate loans that are based on the loan-to-value ratio and the investor's experience. If you do not have experience, working with a seasoned rehabber to close a few deals will position you to get your own funding after you have a few deals under your belt.

Here are the steps to doing a house flip:

1. Find a distressed property well below market value (could be physically distressed or the

owner is under financial distress and needs to sell).

2. Make a cash offer at 65% of the after-repair value.
3. Get a hard money loan for the purchase price and rehab (if bank financing is not available on the property).
4. Get quotes from three contractors on the costs of repairs for the property.
5. Choose a contractor and have them renovate the property (some people do it themselves).
6. Market the property for sale or hire a real estate agent to list the property.
7. Sell and close on the property and if you plan properly, make a large sum of money.

Flipping a house offers many benefits beyond the deal. It offers a family a shiny new home to live in. It beautifies a neighborhood. Let's face it. The vacant house in a community is an eye sore that can bring down the value of a neighborhood. On the other side, a house that is newly remodeled will sell for top dollar and therefore increase the value of the property. While this is a very challenging path in real estate, finding pros who are flipping houses can help you to bridge the learning gap.

Unlocking Real Estate Investing

HOUSE FLIPPING CHECKLIST

Property Street Address: _____

City: _____ State: _____ Zip: _____

First: Submit the Offer

To Do:	Reporting/Software:
Contact Agent and Contractor to Walk Through Property	Inspection Checklist
Walkthrough/Inspect Property for Repairs Needed	Repair Cost Calculator
Complete Inspection Checklist for Preliminary Scope of Work	Minimum Purchase Price Calculator
Determine Preliminary Repair Cost Estimate	Investment Report
Figure Out the Maximum Purchase Price for the Property	Maximum Purchase Price Report
Share Financial Analysis with Partners (if applicable)	Repair Cost Estimate Report
Offer Decision:	Homeowner Offer Report
Make "Yes" or "No" Decision on Offer	**Property Documentation:**
Send Signed Offer/Purchase Agreement to Agent/Seller	MLS Listing Information
Send Copy of EMD/Certified Check (if required)	Comparable Sales Information
Send Proof of Funds Letter (if required)	Tax Information
Offer Tracking:	Signed Purchase Agreement
Offer #1: _____ Counter #1: _____	EMD/Certified Check
Offer #2: _____ Counter #2: _____	Proof of Funds Letter
Accepted Offer: _____ Date: _____	

Second: The Offer Is Accepted

To Do:	Property Documentation:
Send Original Copy of EMD/Proof of Funds (if required)	Signed Purchase Agreement
Schedule a walkthrough/inspection	Contract Addendum
If Financing:	Copy of EMD/Certified Check
Send Property Info, Contact & Closing Date to Lender	
Schedule an Appraisal with the Lender	

Third: Time to do Property Inspections

*Get inspection with professional inspector or contractor to get a detailed scope of work for the property.

Arrange for Utilities to be Turned On for Inspection		Reporting/Software:	
Conduct Property Inspections		Inspection Checklist	
Home Inspection	Structural Evaluation	Scope of Work Report Builder	
Termite Inspection	Radon Evaluation	**Property Documentation:**	
Waste Line Inspection	Abatement Inspection	Final Inspection Report	
Receive Final Inspection Report/Termite Report		Termite Letter	
Create Detailed Scope of Work		Tip: **After walkthrough/property inspection you may be able to make reasonable financial decision to move forward or not. Seek bids for repair.	
**Make a "Yes"/"No" Decision to Purchase Property			
OR solicit BIDS from Contractors			
First: Submit the Offer			

Wholesaling

As you can imagine, finding a property to buy for less than 65% of the value is not the easiest process. That is why many rehabbers turn to wholesalers to find the property for them. Wholesaling is the process of finding a property below market value, getting it into contract with the seller, then selling it below market value without taking ownership of the property.

Successful wholesalers market to distressed sellers using everything from mail, email, and social media. They get paid by securing a contract from the seller at one price and selling the rights to the contract for a higher price. With wholesaling you can literally get started in real estate with no money and no credit because you never actually have to buy a property! While the barrier for entry is low, the competition is high, and the marketing cost can add up.

Wholesaling carries a low risk because you do not have to borrow money on your credit, nor would you be required to put down a large deposit to get into contract. With the drive to succeed and the willingness to work through disappointments and rejection, new real estate investors can get solid paydays by taking this path.

Unlike rental income, wholesaling is not passive income. It is like a job. You would be required to do research to find the property and the sellers who are willing to sell for a low price. You also must find buyers who are willing and capable of closing quickly. Often to get one deal, it can take tons of mailers, hundreds of phone calls, and constantly generating new leads. The market is saturated because it is one of the lower hanging fruits in the real estate investing business. Still, this path has helped many people reach their financial goals.

Being a Private Lender

The Bible says, "A borrower is a slave to the lender." In any city you go to, the tallest buildings have the name of a bank on them. Banking institutions amass wealth by taking money deposited into their bank and lending it to make multiples of the money they brought in. For consumers, receiving 1% or less on their banking accounts is a bad deal, but for the banks, they're laughing all the way to the bank.

What these institutions do can also be done by you. People who are saving money in bank accounts and retirement accounts can be the bank too. Real estate investors are always looking for money for deals. Sometimes they are looking for hundreds of thousands of dollars and other times they are looking for tens of thousands of dollars for smaller deals.

For someone who has been contributing to their IRA and/or 401(k) for 20 years, there is money sitting and making very little interest. With self-directed retirement accounts, regular people like you and I can put these funds to work to make higher rates of returns with real estate deals that meet your risk tolerance.

Real Estate Education

After you have purchased your first home, I hope you get bit by the real estate bug. There are so many different paths to take in the real estate world. The options can be dizzying. Each field is its own course to mastery and wealth. Based on your financial goals there is a space in real estate that can fulfill you. Many people get enthusiastic about real estate after watching an infomercial, or a reality show. From there to make the energy transform into action, there should be steps to learn more.

Educating yourself is essential. Unlike school, the pursuit of knowledge is not going to be graded or monitored. How much you study shows how much you want it. There are many channels to teach you what you want to learn. Since there are so many channels and paths in real estate, take your time to choose which type of real estate you want to start with. I emphasize "start with" because you do not have to marry single family homes, or storage unit investing. You get to try it, and if you like it, do more. If not, try something else. Have the vision you have for your life guide this decision.

Some people like Phil Georges, jumped right into multi-family property. Others like Jantzen Young built their wealth by flipping land and lending money. Khalid from Chapter 5 chose to flip houses. You can be successful in any area of real estate but chasing every good idea in real estate is a recipe for disaster.

To start your education, go to YouTube University. As you know, YouTube holds information about most things you want to know. Real estate is no exception. If you want to buy single family homes to rent out, there are videos that will lead you down a rabbit hole of information on the subject. Again, if you hone-in on one area of focus, you can develop a good understanding of your future journey as a real estate investor.

To take the next step you can go to real estate meetups and events.

Join a REIA

If YouTube University got you hyped about becoming a real estate mogul, the next thing to do is to hang out where many real estate moguls hang out. REIAs are Real Estate Investment Associations.

This is a place where other students of the game go to learn and grow. REIAs are located all over the country and offer networking and education which are essential for expediting your launch into real estate investing.

What you will learn at these meetings is that millionaires can be found in Ferragamos or in old Skechers. When you are in a room of real estate enthusiasts, which a REIA is, you will meet people at all phases of success and all areas of expertise. This is where you can find who you need and learn what you need to make it in real estate. With a focus on what you want to do, you can connect with people who are already doing it. They can offer you resources and insights on how to achieve what they have achieved.

These clubs are a real community and if you join, you will be able to develop relationships that can change your life forever. Look for a Real Estate Investment Association close to you and become a regular.

Keys to Successful Networking

1. Tell everyone what you do and what you are looking for.
2. Listen carefully to what other people do and what they want.

3. Connect people who need each other (i.e., introduce a wholesaler to a rehabber).
4. Collect business cards and contact information.
5. Follow up manually or use a CRM (Customer Relationship Manager).
6. Be generous with contacts and information.
7. Be consistent.
8. Volunteer your time or skills to the organization.

With these steps, your goals will come to you exponentially faster than by trying to get there yourself. Like the African proverb says, "If you want to go fast, go alone, if you want to go far, go together." Fly in a "V" formation with others who are intentionally making progress toward their real estate goals, and you will have support, resources, and access that will make your journey successful.

Real Estate Podcast

Education in real estate is in high demand. There are multiple vessels that allow people to gain the knowledge they crave. Podcasts have emerged as a major way for aspiring real estate millionaires to consume information.

Here is a list of some popular real estate podcasts and shows that can help you to get the information which will take you to the next level in your real estate journey. I have listed some of these shows below.

- Bigger Pockets
- The Money Flippers (Hosted by Jantzen Young and me)
- The Remote Real Estate Investor
- One Rental at a Time
- Real Estate Today Radio
- The Real Estate Guys Radio Show
- Best Real Estate Investing Advice Ever Show
- Apartment Building Investing
- Lifetime Cashflow Through Real Estate Investing
- Cash Flow Guys
- Real Estate News for Investors
- Real Estate Investing Mastery

Blueprint 7

From Homebuyers to Investors
Dr. Alfonso and Daton

Fear is a funny thing. When you believe in it, it can stop you from doing anything. When you overcome it, nothing can stop you from doing anything. Daton was full of fear in 2016 when he started working with me. His belief was his credit was bad, yet the reality was his score was low because he had a maxed-out credit card and no other debt. I worked with him to build his credit quickly, and when that obstacle was out of his way, he took off.

He and his husband, Alfonso, were hard working and committed to buying their first property. They had big dreams and now that credit was not an issue, they decided not to just buy a house, but they chose to go for it and get a multi-family property as their first home.

"Since we bought a multi-family, we were able to have most of our mortgage paid by our tenants. Designing the apartments for us and our tenants helped us uncover our love for interior design. Our first house was the tip of the iceberg. We could only see what was in front of us at the time, but under the surface, real estate has become a passion of ours which allows us to provide beautiful housing for people. We did not know how much that would matter to us until we saw the impact it had on our tenants."

This turned out to be a great opportunity for them, yet it was not at all easy. "Being a perfectionist, I overanalyzed every detail. I was losing sleep over things worrying could not change. Overcoming it put a mirror up to other areas of my life and taught me to trust the people I choose to work with. Also, to trust my partner more, and to trust things would work out, because everything in the process does not have to be so intense and scary. The biggest thing I learned was that something does not have to be easy for you to experience ease." Daton really dropped the mic with that one!

After buying their first house, Daton and Alfonso thought buying a second house just made sense. They were able to buy their first house while Alfonso was in medical school, so they felt confident they could do it again regardless of what challenges would come up. "The process for the second house was much different than the first. Since we already had a multi-family house, we decided to choose the area we wanted to be in as we grew into our next phase of life. We were able to take more risks and be very intentional about what we wanted."

The process for the next house turned out to have more issues, yet with the experience they gained the first time around, as things came up, they said, "We can do this!" Daton said, "With our new house we messed up with a bunch of things. We accepted that we may fail, and how it's really an opportunity to learn. Everything eventually worked out and now we have gone from being renters to owning two properties in a few short years. Now we never stop looking at homes to buy. We have a vision and dream we can go for, and homeownership changed everything for us."

Blueprint to Start Investing in Real Estate

1. Read *Rich Dad Poor Dad* by Robert Kiyosaki.
2. Determine your short-term and long-term real estate goals. Do you want to be an active real estate investor or a passive investor?
3. Work with your lender to determine the lending requirements for your next property.
4. Join your local real estate investment association to learn more about real estate investing.
5. Set a target date to purchase your next property based on your investment strategy.

About the Author

Chad Murray is a best-selling author and an award-winning speaker. He is a lender, and his workshops empower people through the education and resources he shares. His financial literacy company Your Credit Coach, LLC teaches adults and teenagers the power real estate and credit have to change their lives.

At the age of 19, Chad got his start as a mortgage banker, and today he teaches people how to successfully navigate the home buying journey through his online course, Home Buyer's Academy.

As a lender Chad helps first time buyers achieve their home ownership goals, and he is a private lender for real estate investors. Through his lending business, Chad can offer financing for real estate for multiple asset classes and many types of borrowers.

Born and raised in Queens, New York, and proud father of two, Chad now resides in Orlando, Florida.

Scan the QR Code below to set up a home buying consultation or email: hello@chadthelender.com

Made in the USA
Coppell, TX
26 February 2022